An American Adventure in Bookburning

In The Style of 1918

James J. Martin

RM
Ralph Myles Publisher, Inc.
COLORADO SPRINGS

BOOKS by JAMES J. MARTIN —

*Men Against the State: The Expositors of
   Individualist Anarchism in America* (1953, 1970)

American Liberalism and World Politics, 1931-1941
   (2 Volumes, 1964)

*Revisionist Viewpoints: Essays in a Dissident
   Historical Tradition* (1971, 1977)

*The Saga of Hog Island and Other Essays in
   Inconvenient History* (1977)

*Beyond Pearl Harbor: Essays on Some Consequences
   of the Crisis in the Pacific in 1941* (1983)

*The Man Who Invented 'Genocide':
   The Public Career and Consequences of
   Raphael Lemkin* (1984)

*An American Adventure in Bookburning,
   In The Style of 1918* (1989)

An American
Adventure
in
Bookburning

Library of Congress Cataloging-in-Publication Data

Martin, James Joseph, 1916-
    An American adventure in bookburning in the style
of 1918.

    Bibliography: p.
    Includes index.
    1. World War, 1914-1918—Censorship—United States.
2. Soldiers' libraries—Censorship—United States—
History—20th century. I. Title.
D632.M37   1988   303.3'76   89-3246
ISBN 0-87926-024-6

First Edition

Typesetting and design by UniverCity WorDesign, Portland, Oregon.
This book was created on a Macintosh Plus computer with
QuarkStyle™ desktop publishing software.

Ralph Myles Publisher, Inc.
Post Office Box 1533
Colorado Springs, CO 80901 U.S.A.

Contents

An American Adventure in Bookburning

Origins of the Action & Some Related Considerations

On August 31, 1918, a little over two months before the end of the war in Europe, Newton Diehl Baker, Secretary of War in the cabinet of President Woodrow Wilson,[1] issued a directive ordering the removal from U.S. Army camp libraries of 31 publications, most of them published books. Secretary Baker classified these as undesirable reading matter for America's mainly conscripted armed forces located at these posts, forts and other installations large enough to boast a camp library. The vague instructions to camp librarians left it in doubt whether these works by more than 30 authors were to be destroyed or simply removed from the shelves and sequestered from circulation. The explanation as to why they were considered unsuitable reading for the country's soldiery was that they were "German propaganda." Nothing was said about collaboration from the Navy on the application of this prohibition to U.S. naval bases or ships at sea with comparable library facilities.

The interest of the wartime government of President Wilson in the possible reading matter of the citizenry at large had been made very obvious within just a few weeks after Congress put the country at war with Imperial Germany and its allies of the Central Powers on April 6, 1917. It will be shown later that this interest and interference began long before this date, but with belligerence, formal involvement became a matter of official policy. Various classes of internal "subversion" became objects of intense scrutiny, following the enactment by

Congress of the Espionage Act on June 15, 1917, and about nine months later the Sedition Act, passed after an unrecorded vote on March 4, 1918. (Both these actions had additional state supplementation of sorts.) But special attention was devoted to what might be read by the armed forces.

Among the many bureaucracies which were quickly constructed and made operative in the United States upon entering the war as a formal belligerent on April 6 was an elaborate control system over the reading matter of the people who were to do the fighting. It was structured within the American Library Association, and was called the War Library Service (WLS).[2] It had its own staff but came under the authority of the Director of this Service, who was also the Librarian of Congress, Dr. Herbert Putnam, and was based in the Library of Congress, its operational headquarters. The announcement of the suppressed books by order of the Secretary of War came from this headquarters address in the form of a circular letter addressed to all camp librarians.

In actuality, the list of forbidden books had been anticipated about three weeks earlier by the announcement of the banning of five titles, and a directive to Army camp librarians from the WLS head, Dr. Putnam, on August 9, alerting them that "pacifist pamphlets" were being left around at random on library premises. It ended by urging the librarians to "please watch for them and destroy them." The original five titles were added to the bottom of the list issued August 31, and which was ultimately to be expanded with an amended list 3-1/2 weeks later, as will be seen.

A full column story with four separate headlines greeted this action by the War Department in the New York *Times* on September 1.[3] It also included the complete list of the books and authors, including the mistakes in both titles and names of authors, but without any details as to publishers and dates of publication, in actuality omissions of critical importance. Following is the list as it appeared in the *Times* story, which was subsequently reproduced about the country far and wide in other newspapers:

E.G. Balch — *Approaches to the Peace Settlement*
Alexander Berkman — *Prison Memoirs of an Anarchist*
John W. Burgess — *America's Relation to the Great War*

"   " — *European War of 1914*
Capshaw Carson — *Witness Testifies*
Arthur G. Daniells — *World in Perplexity*
"   " — *World War*
A.H. Granger — *England's World Empire*
Frank Harris — *England or Germany*
Sven Hedin — *With the German Armies in the West*
E.F. Henderson — *Germany's Fighting Machine*
Frederic G. Howe — *Why War?*
Roland G. Higgins — *Germany Misjudged*
Rufus M. Jones — *A More Excellent Way*
W.S. Leake — *How to Protect Our Soldiers*
I.T.T. Lincoln — *Revelations of An International Spy*
M.E. Macaulay — *Germany in War Time*
James K. McGuire — *What Could Germany Do for Ireland?*
H. von Muecke — *Emden*
Hugo Muensterberg — *The War in America*
Ernst zu Reventlow — *The Vampire of the Continent*
F.F. Schrader — *German-American Handbook*
Margaret Skinnider — *Doing My Bit for Ireland*
M.M. Thomas and others — *Conquest of War*
George Sylvester Viereck — *Songs of Armageddon*
Anonymous — *World's Crises in the Light of Prophecy*
Anonymous — *Free Speech and a Free Press*
Edmund von Mach — *What Germany Wants*
Seumas MacManus — *Ireland's Case*
Scott Nearing — *Open Letters to Profiteers*
Theodora Wilson Wilson — *The Last Weapon*

By far the greatest attention to this censorship incident occurred in New York City, as *Times* reporters tried to find out the motivation for it all, and to learn what was in these particular books which caused the Government to target them for impounding or destruction.

The New York state headquarters of the American Library Association, then located at 134 East 28th Street, was unable to furnish any information at all, but tried to explain what had been going on the previous year or so with regard to the reading interests of the American servicemen and how it had all been handled.

The American Library Association had been the sole organization designated to distribute books and magazines to the personnel of the armed forces. These were obtained by purchase and also by collection of donated materials from the general public. The ALA depended in part upon other organizations such as the YMCA and the Knights of Columbus, and other relief and service groups, to make books avail-

9

able which were first gathered by the Library War Service of the ALA. As of the end of August 1918, in barely a year of operation, there had been collected as gifts from the citizenry over 3,000,000 books for service libraries.

It was in the course of learning this that reporters suggested that this may have been the way in which "German propagandists" might have infiltrated "pro-German" literature into servicemens' hands. This was their fishing expedition, of course, since no official explanation had accompanied the banning order. But, since an alert had already been issued concerning pacifist works, which were obviously not the same thing, it seemed logical to suggest that there may have been several reasons for this censorship action. Other marked works were possible "seditious" treatises, as legally defined, and hostile political tracts by people who simply opposed the war without favoring the war adversary in any particular way.

Responding to this, Edwin H. Anderson, of the New York Public Library and a member of the War Service Committee of the ALA, and others, maintained that there was a close watch made on contributed books, that camp libraries were supplied only with volumes which had passed this process of examination and selection. Furthermore, they had no information or evidence that the forbidden tomes were actually among the accessions of any camp library anywhere. All they had to work on was the previous alert as to the finding of "pamphlets of a seditious or pacifist nature" which had been "surreptitiously placed on the open shelves of the [camp] libraries without the knowledge of the librarians."

When Anderson was further questioned as to whether any of the "War Department's Index" were to be found in any libraries of the New York City system, he said he did not know the answer to that either. But he did volunteer that they might very well have been a part of the reference shelves "for research students"; "If Satan wrote a pro-German book, we should want it for our reference shelves," Anderson commented, remarking that "It might be of use to future historians." But he concluded that "in the circulating department we exclude all pro-German books, and have done so since the beginning [sic] of the war. We go over the books from time to time and take out those that are objectionable." So what appeared to be a matter of purely armed forces interest and concern was obviously being put into a civilian context at once; in a war situation there did not appear to be any separation between the military and civilian worlds one might have been expected to see prevail in theory.

There were two aspects of Mr. Anderson's response to the reporters which one might have thought would have led to additional reportorial queries. Since the "beginning" of which war had the librarians started removing and concealing "pro-German" books from library users: that beginning in August, 1914 or the phase commencing with American involvement in April, 1917? It suggested that the library people had taken upon themselves a censorship task which no one seemed to be aware of, and one which did not stem from some official government ukase; no one recalled that Washington had authorized libraries to perform such a censorship chore.

The second element of Mr. Anderson's reply which should have aroused reportorial curiosity was the volunteered revelation that the object of this program of book removal consisted of "pro-German" books. How this was determined was of major importance, and not a word of explanation followed nor was any requested. What constituted "pro-German" and whose opinions on this became operational policy? An incredible opportunity for abuse existed here, and someone's subjective idiosyncrasy obviously could have swelled the total of suppressed books immensely without a particle of proof having to be advanced as to the "pro-German" content of any of them. In view ultimately of the wide spread of subjects encompassed by the War Department's decree affecting Army libraries, all arranged under the tent of "pro-German" propaganda, the door appeared to have been opened to book-suppressors of a vast range of views and convictions to have impounded their pet dislikes under the over-all scatter-gun identification of "pro-German," without the faintest possibility for the establishment of formal protest or objection. Looked at from this point of view, the right to read of the civilian community was if anything in worse danger at the hands of the public librarians in the civilian sector than was the recognizably circumscribed right of a member of the armed forces in a service library.

It is obvious that if we take the original action by Secretary Baker in context, this move against books instead of people produced an

11

immediate effect on civilians which was apparently unanticipated, but the counter argument may be made that it should have been logically expected. Though the proscribed books were specifically targeted for removal from the libraries of Army establishments exclusively, what followed suggested that some related action was also expected if not assumed on the part of those administering the libraries of the citizenry at large. There occurred almost immediately pressure on public librarians to emulate the action of Army post libraries from the mysterious but seemingly omnipresent organization known as the American Defense Society. At this point this account would be illuminated by an elaboration.

It is probable that only in America is it likely that anyone would encounter something such as the American Defense Society. This body (like its counter-part, the National Security League) was not an official part of the Government whatever. But it behaved like one, if it did not actually exceed one in its zeal. A super-watchdog over the land, it consisted of private citizens and various volunteer civilian auxiliaries of the formal machinery of the police and governmental regulatory bodies, but with a special urgent appetite for the prosecution of Mr. Wilson's war. If anyone anticipated the general concept of "total war," it was this apparatus, which became active about two weeks after the commencement of formal hostilities and American involvement. It developed a hefty portfolio of views, opinions and policies on almost everything related to the prosecution of the war and the maintenance of properly belligerent attitudes among the general citizenry. And it was in the forefront in advancing the most aggravating and socially incendiary views on the suppression of outlooks on the war not in accord with the most warlike expressions to be found anywhere.

It particularly sought to suppress or to uproot all aspects of German culture still surviving in the U.S.A., including its press, and pointedly even the teaching of the German language in the schools. This strange crusade against the total background of America's second largest ethnic group managed to reach preposterous levels.

The ADS organization developed "chapters" in a large number of U.S. communities, tended to be anonymous in that specific persons were frequently not identified when its pronouncements appeared in newspapers, and managed to conceal any objectives it may have had other than its obvious function, as self-defined, prosecution of total war on the home front as they hoped it also was at the war fronts. But occasionally it could not conceal its ties to elements which were finding the war very profitable along with whatever other objectives were being realized.

Such figures at its top who did manage to be identified at various times during the war did not exactly strike one as what might have been called household names of the time. This was true during the last eight months of 1917. But things changed a bit when former President Theodore Roosevelt consented to become its honorary national director in January, 1918.[4] Newspapers of that time had got into the habit of calling him "Colonel" Roosevelt, perhaps a concession to his preference and to his tendency to exploit a military title in a time of a popular war. But this was as close to the military as the American Defense Society was to get. And it savored the war as few others did, maintaining itself at top emotion to the end of hostilities, and, for that matter, well beyond, being involved in domestic politics as late as 1922.

In view of their enthusiasm for the war, it was understandable that sentiments in favor of peace or expectations or desires of a halting of hostilities were imperceptible if at all in existence. Their commitment for the long haul, no matter how long it might be, was reflected in their activities and devotion to persistence in deepening the war psychology by all means, in their ranks. Their conviction that the war was going to last for a goodly spell was commonplace well down through 1918; the suspension of fighting and the Armistice of November 11 must have come as a shock to many members. That the war might go on at least three and perhaps five more years had been taken for granted by leaders and the general run of membership alike. Their new chief, "Colonel" Roosevelt, on March 28, 1918 expressed the view that combat was very likely to last well into 1921 and thought that the Wilson Administration should be planning to put into the field an army of 5,000,000.[5] This is not the place for an extended narrative about the American Defense Society, but only to deal in part with its involvement eventually in applying the Army book-burning adventure to the civilian sector, something which got extremely little attention. But one may comment that when Charles E. Montague wrote in his postwar book *Disenchantment* (1922) that "War hath no fury like a non-combatant," he could not possibly have described more succinctly the American Defense Society.

What the Department of the Army established for military personnel in wartime was obviously its own business, and if it decreed that certain books were not to be read by people in uniform while in its employ and on its premises, it was entirely proper for it to act in this way. But when this program spread immediately and directly to the remainder of the national community, it became quite obviously everybody else's business. And here is where it became a gross lapse on the part of the general citizenry to do nothing whatever, or, if anything, to cooperate in their own intellectual hijacking, by standing by or actually aiding and assisting the American Defense Society in sweeping clean and sterilizing the shelves of their local public libraries in accord with the dictates of the Department of the Army through indirection, probably, but just as thoroughly as though deliberately undertaken.

The American Defense Society leaped into this new phase of suppression by cracking down on the community's possible intellectual interests with alacrity, though action varied from place to place, some having their libraries sanitized before others. It became apparent that Secretary Baker's office had no reluctance whatever in furnishing the local chapters of the ADS with the list of proscribed works. Then influence was applied to local library boards to have librarians remove these titles from the book stacks under their jurisdiction. When this action was initiated, response to it sometimes was almost immediate.[6] The reason for the headlong haste to comply with this kind of psychic intimidation has not been probed, since the American Defense Society did not have a gram of legal authority to impose its desires on anybody, and no one was under the faintest compulsion even to notice that they were in existence.

It should be understood that when Secretary Baker took the Army Department into the tangled thickets of literary suppression late in 1918, it was not the first time a department of Mr. Wilson's government had essayed forth in this capacity. The Justice Department had been at it for 16 months by that time, on a formal basis. And there eventually was evidence put on the record that well before American involvement in the war, Justice and various other agencies of the Government had been in one surreptitious way or another interfering or meddling in the citizenry's reading matter and interests, in behalf of various possible clients or beneficiaries, even if quite unofficially.

It is instructive to pay some attention to at least part of this experience of the Justice Department in the pursuit of forbidden books prior to the Army adventure, for at least three reasons: 1) to give a student of it all an idea of what the Army had got into in the light of what Justice was still going through on its own initiative in this field; 2) to indicate the muddled and overlapping nature of the various efforts in this enterprise, as well as the confusion in coping with the total problem created by this intellectual invasion by the Government as to jurisdiction when possibly derived from three separate acts of Congress in dealing with such citizens as defied the Government in these matters, for whatever reason; 3) to envisage what lay in store for the authorities in the general civilian community when they took up the burden of banned-book-chasing as a consequence of collaborating with the Army's self-appointed enforcers, the American Defense Society. (It was fortunate for the Army Department that the war ended so soon after this entire operation was instituted.)

Though there were people convicted under the Espionage and the Sedition Acts, as well as the Selective Service Act (May 18, 1917), who were in some cases still in prison four years after the end of the shooting phase of the war, we know little about the fate of outlawed literature *in toto,* how much of it was impounded, how much destroyed, what publishers coerced into abandoning various works in whatever stage of production, and many other substantive circumstances of this kind. But prior to analyzing the content of the books on the celebrated Army list, it might help to understand the problem by examining in detail the saga of one title not on their list which lay entirely within the scope of the operations of the Justice Department. One of the proscribed titles on the earliest Army list was the anonymously written *World's Crisis in the Light of Prophecy* (the Army listing had pluralized one word into "Crises.") The title gave the impression of being a work issued by the dynamic new religious sect known as the "Russellites," as well as by half a dozen other names (they were not to be called the Jehovah's Witnesses until 1931.) Actually it was a publication of a rival group with many similar views, the Seventh

15

Day Adventists, but it reminded those keeping track of this aspect of ideological conflict of the former, and the incredible course of affairs involving one of their books, *The Finished Mystery*. The absence of this book from Secretary Baker's list and the inclusion of other far less formidable volumes by other religious minorities with lukewarm or hostile attitudes toward the war must have caused other departments in Mr. Wilson's government to wonder what was going on, as the sensational and continuing affair involving this work convinced many of those involved that if there was one book at large in the land in late 1918 which the war's prosecutors might have wanted to keep out of military libraries it was *The Finished Mystery,* and it had absolutely nothing to do with any sympathy with the war adversary.

Charles Taze Russell (1852-1916), the founder of the bible study group which bore his name for several decades, had scored one of the great windfalls of prediction as far back as 1877 when he prophesied that a catastrophic era of turmoil would strike the world beginning in 1914, at which time also would begin "the end of Satan's period of uninterrupted rule of the earth."

Russell's movement gained momentum and membership steadily and had a strong base by the time of his demise on October 31, 1916, after which he was succeeded early in January, 1917 by Judge Joseph F. Rutherford, during whose early tenure the group began to obtain sensational publicity. Already known for the immense size of the print runs of their publications, this policy was vastly augmented under Judge Rutherford. And it was under his direction that there took place a collation of the unpublished writings of their deceased founder. Compiled by C.J. Woodworth and G.H. Fisher, it became a 608-page hardbound book selling for 60¢ postpaid, issued at noon on July 17, 1917,[7] a little over three months after U.S. entry into World War One. Its uncompromising criticism of patriotism and related nationalistic sentiments as "a certain delusion" and the war itself as "a work of Satan," along with other political views shocking to commonly-held sensibilities, guaranteed that it would be a prime target for political suppression.

But it was not that easy. Though the Justice Department swiftly took off after *The Finished Mystery,* as well as everyone who was identified with its distribution and sale, not just its publisher, the book spread like dry leaves in a strong wind. By the end of August, 1917 there were 850,000 copies around, and the Russellites claimed that its sale "was unparalleled by the sale of any other book known, in the same length of time, excepting the Bible."

The Russellites repeatedly insisted that this book had been planned long before American involvement in the war. It is not known how many copies were in existence by the end of 1917, on the last day of which year, in addition to the book itself, there took place a mass distribution of 10,000,000 copies of a tract which contained several of the more incitatory views in *The Finished Mystery* on the war. It was hard to imagine anyone not having at least heard of this matter as governmental action against the publisher began to get serious early in 1918.

The full story of this event would be a massive tome. But for the purposes of this study it is sufficient to concentrate on a few highlights. There were close to ten thousand of the movement's believers involved in distributing this book, and it was obvious that the Government's efforts at censorship were little more than a sensational fiasco. Pressure on the publisher led variously from excision of various pages from the book to an agreement to suspend further distribution, though at the same time there were continued protests against this hostile action, even to President Wilson himself. A mass mailing of one of their periodicals, *Kingdom News, No. 2* dated April 15, 1918 bore a streamer headline *"The Finished Mystery* and Why Suppressed," and went to a vast international audience. On May 1 came *Kingdom News, No. 3* and with that the heavy hand of the Government fell.

A week later Judge Rutherford and seven associates were arrested.[8] Tried beginning on June 3, they were sentenced to 20 years each in federal prison on June 21, 1918,[9] and spent approximately nine months in the federal penitentiary in Atlanta. Released on appeal after paying bail in early March, 1919 their conviction was overturned on May 14, 1919 by a federal appeals court, while the entire judgment and action was dismissed May 5, 1920 when the Government decided not to re-prosecute. In the meantime, with the end of the war, immense numbers of stockpiled copies of *The Finished Mystery* poured out across the country (there had in addition been a special edition issued on March 1, 1918), and the dissolution of the Government's suit was greeted six weeks later (June 21, 1920) by a massive paperback edition.

And in a breath-taking gesture of defiance and re-assertion of their belief in their original correctness, as well as a swift repudiation of the prestigious Federal Council of Churches, whom the Russellites believed had approved of their persecution during 1917-1919, Judge Rutherford's group in an immense convention in Cedar Point, Ohio on September 8, 1922 issued a pronunciamento backing their stand on the war and launching a withering view on the Council's postwar politics as well. In January, 1919 the Council had vociferously acclaimed the League of Nations (which the U.S.A. did not join) as "the political expression of the Kingdom of God on earth." The September 8, 1922 Russellite resolution not only castigated the mainline American clergy for the "disloyalty" by their "participation in the war," but dismissed the Council's international politics, expressing the conviction, "all international conferences and all agreements or treaties resulting therefrom, including the League of nations compact and all like compacts, must fail."[10] They then proceeded to print and distribute a stunning edition of 35,000,000 copies of it all, and spread them across the world.

There is no comparable *denouement* to an adventure in the attempted suppression of the printed word as what was brought about by the Russellites between 1919 and 1922. Perhaps the Army thought what the Justice Department was doing, 1917-1918, to make life miserable for them was sufficient, and no need existed to list their provocative book among their forbidden anthology. But, as in the case of other omissions, absence implied at least indifference, if not indirect assumption of innocent contents, as far as the sensibilities of the military were concerned. Whether Secretary Baker and his people were learning anything while this was going on is indeterminable, but they obviously were in a political and legal position where they could have left the pursuit of authors, publishers and books to other agencies in the land.

Prior to an investigation via content analysis of the famed Army list of proscribed books, as well as directing some attention to their authors, who if anything got less at the time they became notorious than at the time what they wrote had been first published, a few additional observations of a general nature seem to be called for. Though the New York City journalists tried at the time of first publicity to establish why the first collection were being banned, they really did not succeed, even if it was obvious that a mixture of the substantive and political was involved. But the advancement of the excuse that their unsuitability for a servicemen reading audience was simply that they were "German propaganda"[11] did not satisfy the inquisitive. The latter were able to establish even on a superficial basis that several of the authors had produced works which had nothing to do with German objectives, and that persons of German citizenship or extraction were a small minority of the total. But there were no real contemporary investigations or analyses of the books or their writers, and the entire thing tended to be taken from that time on at its face value.

Still another aspect which ranged from the opaque to the muddy as far as understanding was concerned was the relationship of the publishing business to all this. Though about half of the list consisted of tomes with exotic sponsorship, the other half had been launched by some of the country's most prestigious firms, and had been around for years, as will be subsequently dwelled upon. A little more background may help here as well.

A clause in the Espionage Act of 1917 gave the Post Office Department via the Postmaster General's personal power of scrutiny very wide discretion in denying the use of the mails by and clearing the mails of magazines and newspapers which carried hostile views of Mr. Wilson's war. The wartime news channels (there was neither radio nor television then) were filled with endless seizure stories and the prosecution and jailing of publishers and others involved in circulating these types of printed materials. In the process, among several other achievements, America's German language periodical press was essentially destroyed. However there is very little dealing with the effect of these censorship activities on books and book publishers, even it one spectacular case has already been examined, above.

Though mail seizures took place in their case as well, much of what the Wilson interception and censorship machinery found objectionable had been printed well prior to American belligerency, and the work of suppression which was done in these areas was mainly of an *ex post facto* nature.

The first stage of this rooting out of objectionable printed sources coincided with the pursuit and repression both of speakers and of public speeches (circulated in printed form subsequently) which also opposed for one reason or another the wartime Government's policies. Early emphasis was on resistance to conscription and related war moves, and the majority of the first wave of prosecutions were of radicals: anarchists, socialists, syndicalists, and various pacifists and a scattering of religious leaders with related views.

But the direction taken when the Army Department began its offensive in September, 1918 was a counter-move of a branch of the Government against the intellectual interests of a broad spectrum of the citizenry, in actuality, since the books it ordered purged from Army post libraries, and which deletions swiftly spread to public libraries in the civilian world at large and at random, represented a wide variety of interests, only a few of which had any real relation to the alleged subject, "German propaganda." When the original list of 31 was joined by a new one of 16 additional titles filed by Secretary Baker on September 25, 1918 there was somewhat less curiosity aroused. No publicity was given to the titles this time, though seven authors were identified, and only the title of a symposium was published.[12]

A few other general conclusions should be made at this point. There were no follow-up accounts revealing that any of these 47 published works were ever found in an Army or Navy camp or ship library. In fact there were no quantitative reports ever publicized on the frequency with which these works were located in the public library system nationwide either. (About half of these titles proved to be extremely hard to find, even in their heyday, but the other half, roughly, were nationally distributed.)

Still another aspect of this curious episode, probably the most disturbing aspect of it all, was the almost total lack of intellectual concern over it, and what might be termed general impassive indifference in the community as such. This encourages another speculation: could the general run of conscript have been able to read and/or understand the banned literature in the first place? It might have been argued with some conviction that educational levels were such that the very largest part of it would have been incomprehensible, and some of the works with mystical religious import simply unintelligible to any without a knowledge of the special terminology employed. For that matter, the high levels at which many of these items were pitched intellectually and culturally indicated that there was a rather slim percentage of the total community with the educational and literacy capability of grasping more than a smattering of the content involved; the educational attainments of several of the authors supported this generalization. Therefore, if one wishes to entertain the dark suspicion that the civilian community was the long-range, delayed-action target of this adventure to begin with, such person would have to deal with this aspect at the same time: who in the population at large would have been able to read from this list with profit, and with sufficient comprehension to be influenced by it?

Prior to the analysis of the famed book list by author and subject matter, it is pertinent to make a general inquiry on the basis of internal evidence as to the source of at least some of the initiative and dynamism behind the go-ahead in the preparation of this literary prohibition. Date of publication and availability of several of these banned titles suggest that concern for purely American sensibilities was a secondary factor. It did not take too acute powers of discovery or analysis to detect that several of the sequestered volumes did not deal with sympathy or support for German objectives at all. And one very peculiar aspect emerged from just a cursory application of investigation to the Secretary of War's Index of Politically Prohibited Books. Three of the titles dealt only in the most distant way with the war in Europe: they concerned internal *Irish* politics.

And this gave rise to speculation as to one possible source for the inspiration behind the action in the first place: the tireless and omnipresent British Intelligence organization's propaganda operation, and their multitude of native American supporters and assistants. The British war government had been since Easter Monday of 1916 engaged in a bloody repression of a full-scale Irish revolt, the latest phase of centuries of trouble keeping Ireland a subordinate part of the United Kingdom, so-called. There did exist the possibility of German support for the Irish upheaval, along the line of the thinking that the enemy of your enemy is in effect your friend. In that sense only might the prohibition of reading about it all have been estimated to be an assist to the German adversary's propaganda. But the total effect obviously was aimed at providing political comfort to the British wartime regime in its two-front war, since the diversion of British military power to suppress and police thereafter the Irish rebellionists obviously detracted from the total force it might have been able to apply to the Western Front in northern France. (From a geopolitical point of view it might have been argued that the situation in Ireland involved British military deployment theoretically over as large an area as was called for on the Western Front, where combined Anglo-Franco-American operations were really confined to what amounted to only about the northern 10% of France and a small strip of Belgium.)

It may have been that few Americans in the closing weeks of the war were interested in the vast scope of British propaganda activities in the U.S.A., though for sure a great many well knew about it, even if then or even 20 years later there was not too great an understanding of it. Begun in the earliest period of American neutrality under the direction of Sir Gilbert Parker, and reorganized in 1917 under Lord Northcliffe, aided by the Pilgrim Society and a vast speakers' bureau, as many as eight different agencies, according to Harold D. Lasswell, pounded away on American sensibilities for 33 months, and may have spent in the U.S.A. throughout the war, 1914-1918, in terms of late 1980s dollars the equivalent of $1 billion setting up Americans for participation in the war on Britain's side. Porter Sargent, a student of this business for over a quarter of a century, concluded that both Sir Gilbert and Lord Northcliffe had profound contempt for American intelligence, considered Americans to be little more critical than sheep, and thought them more gullible than any other people in the world except the Chinese, on whom the yarn was perpetrated that the Germans were boiling down the bodies of their dead soldiers with which to make soap. Though this hoax, described by one of its most careful students as the "most flagrant manufactured atrocity story" of the entire war, was admitted by the British General John Charteris in 1925, it has continued in the *sub rosa* folklore; an astounding example in fiction is to be found in *The Cross of Carl*, by Walter Owen (London: Grant Richards / Fronto Limited, 1931). There are excellent examinations of it all in relation to its original Far East targeted objective in J. Duane Squires, *British Propaganda at Home and in the United States, 1914-1917* (Cambridge, Mass.: Harvard University

Press, 1935) and James Morgan Read, *Atrocity Propaganda, 1914-1919* (New Haven, Conn.: Yale University Press, 1941). (For various aspects of the war for American affections and involvement in World War One, including the references to many specialized studies made in propaganda analysis of that time, one should see especially the many discussions of it in Sargent, *Getting US Into War* [Boston, 1941], pp. 33, 97-8, 101, 107, 111, 132-3, 136, 155, 161-2, 165, 168, 180, 308, 356, 528, 545 and elsewhere.)

In dealing with the book-suppression follies of the War Department in the closing weeks of World War One, then, one must contend with the internal indications that there must have been substantial input derived from cooperation with one or more arms of the British intelligence service operating in the U.S.A., and the suppressed titles dealing critically with Irish affairs and the British Empire (about which more later), are just part of the putative evidence. There is also the implication that this list had been in preparation for some time and was not the result of some impulsive and capricious whim. That it actually fell very far short of being comprehensive is another matter; really diligent "propaganda" sleuths could easily have more than doubled it. The absence even of books known long before American entry in the war to have been subsidized by the German Embassy is just one of many weakness which can be compiled.

We may now begin the examination of the authors and the specific works they produced which ended up on the barred list as well as some by them which did not, and consideration of reasons why they did or did not achieve that status. In addition are included speculations concerning related matters which their citation led to, and further ruminations as to how some authors made the list when no publicity was accorded their product in question (this applies particularly to the writers of the amended list of 16 titles which Army camp librarians were given but which got no further publicity).

Emphasis will be not on what may be found today in literary historical works concerning these authors and publications, but on what was known about both *at that time*. (In most cases there was somewhat more known about the writers 70 years ago than is generally available now.) There will be substantial variations in these commentaries, due to the immense differences among the authors. Some were so obscure that no evidence could be found in ponderous reference compilations that their work had ever been formally issued. In several cases the banned publications were the only things they were known to have published. On the other hand, the professors, and the journalists and other professional writers, were authors of scores of books, and magazine and newspaper pieces almost too numerous to count. Why only one, or perhaps two, of their vast output made this forbidden category thus becomes a subject for additional speculation. The futility of the proscription in the light of their immense additional productivity, and the unconscious lapse on the part of the proscribers in indirectly approving of whatever the targeted writer had produced in addition, even on the same subject, elsewhere, and at another time, as as a result of their superficial approach to the subject, becomes apparent.

The Books and the Authors

Emily Greene Balch (1867-1961) was a veteran and determined pre-war pacifist, partially involved in the famed 1915 Henry Ford "peace ship" endeavor, and had for some time previous been a professor of economics at the exclusive womens' college, Wellesley, in Massachusetts, from which she had been dismissed for her pacifist activities. Her *Approaches to the Great Settlement* (the Army list had substituted the word "Peace" for "Great" in her title) was a substantial work of 351 pages published that same year (1918) by the influential New York firm of B.W. Huebsch, and was decorated by an introduction by an already formidable English figure in peace activity, Norman Angell (1874-1967), which might have been part of the reason the book made the Secretary of War's list. As Sir Norman Angell he was to be awarded the Nobel Peace Prize in 1933. Balch was also to be so honored ultimately, sharing this prize with John R. Mott in 1946. That her book could have been construed as "German propaganda" was hard to figure out, as it contained several references sharply critical of Germany, though the compilers may have reasoned that since it did not support the war, then it must have been produced to afford comfort to the enemy of the moment.

In view of action already taken against Angell, however, the situation would appear that Balch and Angell were jointly objects of pursuit and suppression, and Angell's performing the chore of introducing still another work in this same year of 1918 had drawn him additional attention. Angell's 60-page pamphlet titled *Why Freedom Matters*, prepared and printed some time in the late winter of 1917-1918 by the National Civil Liberties Bureau, was confiscated by the Post Office Department in March, 1918 and ordered destroyed, which made it extremely scarce, as only a few hundred were thought to have been distributed. Then Angell added more fuel to the fire by writing still another introduction to still another annoying work, the book *What Is National Honor? The Challenge of the Reconstruction*, by an unknown writer, Leo Perla, but issued by an industry giant, Macmillan (1918). Though the latter work did not end up on any list of either Post Office, Justice or Army Departments, its substance indicated it may have escaped mainly as a consequence of someone's oversight. (In the second edition of *Webster's New Twentieth Century Unabridged Dictionary*, two of the longest entries, amounting to about three full columns, are devoted to definitions of the words "honor" and "national." However, no attempt is made to define "national honor" in either. After studying Perla's own tortured and confused attempt to define "national honor" in a manner which might have been acceptable all around, in the closing part of his book, one might be excused for coming to the conclusion that it was an impossibility.) There is not much doubt that the ongoing endeavors of Balch and Angell had fairly well etched themselves in the consciousness of the censors and the new thought police. Angell's pre-American-involvement book, *The Dangers of Half-Preparedness* (New York: Putnam, 1916), which caused quite a stir at the time, may have been forgotten, but Balch for sure was memorialized for good as a result of her prominence in the peace agitation of the 1914-1915 International Conference of Women as well as in the 1915 Ford "peace ship." (On the latter one should try to consult the book by the young reporter who was involved in this adventure, Burnet Hershey, *"Get The Boys Out of the Trenches"* [New York: Pyramid Books edition, 1968], especially valuable for its many contemporary photographs and cartoons.)

The real anomaly on the list was Alexander Berkman's *Prison Memoirs of An Anarchist*. Completed in the summer of 1911 (see

25

Emma Goldman, *Living My Life*, 2 vols. [New York: Knopf, 1931], v. 1, p. 483), it had been published in 1912 (New York: Mother Earth Publishing Association). It concerned primarily an event which dated back to 1892 and its aftermath. Berkman had made an attempt to assassinate the steel magnate Henry Clay Frick in that year during the Homestead Steel strike, and subsequently spent a long term in prison upon conviction for that, which was what the book was about. It may be that he ended up on the list on general principles, since he was now back in prison following arrest and prosecution for his efforts in seeking to interfere with the operation of the conscription law of the wartime Government the year before. But here the allegation of "German propaganda" attached to this volume simply defied common sense.

The inclusion of two of the books by Professor Burgess seemed to be the result of delayed discovery, or delayed action based on an existing file. A sober and informed writer of European history and politics and at one time a member of the Columbia University faculty, his books *European War of 1914: Its Causes, Purposes and Probable Results*, and *America's Relation to the Great War*, had appeared in 1915 and 1916, respectively, issued by the major Chicago publisher, A.C. McClurg. They were essential academic treatises which dealt with the war in a detached way appropriate to an observer who was a resident and a citizen of a then-neutral land. They obviously lacked the zeal that the super-heated days of involvement as of the late summer of 1918 called for, as the closing campaigns in France were being successfully fought by the "Allies." Why anyone in an army camp would be reading these early examinations of the war at this late moment was a good question to ask, but undoubtedly the previous reputation of the books was the issue; Professor Burgess was suspected of having been subsidized by the German Embassy and his books tilted in behalf of German views, though almost any book written in the period of U.S. neutrality might have given this impression three years or so later unless it was an overtly pro-British call for "victory," which also proliferated long before American belligerency.

If there had been a prize for the most baffling book on the Army list it surely should have gone to *A Witness Testifies* (the article "A" was left off the title, which should have changed its impact on anyone ignorant of and curious about it substantially). As it turned out, almost any reader would have remained as mystified as before as to what the pseudonymous author, "Capshaw Carson," had "witnessed," and what he might have "testified." This book also deserved a special prize in that the pseudonymous appellation of the author extended to its *publisher* as well: ("Carson Bros. Publishing Co., 623-633 So. Wabash Ave., Chicago").

A wandering, repetitive and outrageously contradictory work the point of which was never made, it took outstanding powers of determined concentration to stick with it through the endless leaps from one position to another. What it had to do with "German propaganda" simply escapes the most meticulous examination. There are in fact several passages in it which not only do *not* assist the enemy but could have been reprinted by the U.S. Committee on Public Information as propaganda *against* the Germans (*e.g.*, pp. 269-282, and elsewhere). Published in January, 1918, even the Library of Congress did not have a copy for some time, while the ponderous and authoritative *United States Catalog* fails even to list it as a published work in the volume covering 1918-1921. It is indeed a strange mélange of mystico-psychologico-sociology, seasoned with a few superficial political opinions, a work which one must read to believe such a labor made the printed media.

In the case of the works of 60-year-old Arthur Grosvenor Daniells, one should link these to a previously-mentioned title, anonymously-issued *World's Crisis in the Light of Prophecy* (1917), partially garbled by the Army; by pluralizing it as "Crises" in its release to the press, they confused it with a "World's Crisis Series" being published through the war, of which it was just one volume. This, and the two books by Daniells, *World War: Its Relation to the Eastern Question and Armageddon* (1917) and *World in Perplexity* (1918), along with another anonymous release, *World Peace in the Light of Bible Prophecy* (1919), were part of this "Crisis" series, all of identical length (128 pages), and all issued by the Review and Herald Publication Association, with various addresses in New York, Washington and South Bend, Indiana. This firm was formally known as one of a network of printing and publishing establishments owned by the Seventh Day Adventists, whose outlook on the war was very similar to the Russellites, objectionable politically for its explicit millenarian approach.[13] Someone concerned with Army fighting morale must have concluded that these books, which looked on the war in Europe as the precursor of the arrival of biblical Armageddon and the imminent Second Coming, were hardly to be construed as contributing to Army enthusiasm for fighting in behalf of one or more worldly governments, even those which basked in the light of such heavenly support as those of Britain, France and the United States, as asserted in such stentorian tones by the legion of divines who helped promote their propaganda.

(In perhaps the most impressive martial demonstration by civilians in history, the sensational "preparedness" parade in New York City on May 13, 1916,[14] over 125,000 people marched without a break for 12 continuous hours, led at various points by 250 brass bands and drum corps, in behalf of increased military involvement nationally. Though the largest contingent consisted of bankers and brokers representing Wall Street, that which got the largest applause along the way were the participating marching phalanx of 130 clergymen, designated by some enthusiasts as the "Church Militant." The main line religious congregations certainly made up for the lack of involvement of the evangelicals and the fundamentalists. Elements ostensibly eager to arm the U.S.A. to the maximum continued to march in scores of other cities in the next few weeks, perhaps as many as a million eventually getting into the streets. But during all this concern for armament, aided previously by the saturating of the country with the immense scare book, *Defenseless America*, by Hudson Maxim,[15] the famed inventor and producer of high explosives who took part in the parade, the U.S. Army fell short of reaching its authorized full complement by 20,000 men, and no inducement or blandishment seemed to work to get this number of additional volunteers. The "finest hour" of the civilians and the martial clergy was to be arrived at a year later, however, following the April 6, 1917 declaration of war. Ray Hamilton Abrams was to memorialize the warriors of the cloth in his book *Preachers Present Arms* (1933), and several others have done justice at least in part to the multitudes of belligerent civilians who never were to hear a shot fired in anger through the period of American involvement. But the pursuit of books by religious minorities out of harmony with the war as late as two weeks before the end of the firing is an indication of something which defies explanation.)

The two critical treatments of the British Empire on the Secretary of War's list which suddenly became "German propaganda" were both published in the U.S.A. in 1916, though the second in alphabetical order was really a book by a German citizen which circulated widely in Germany prior to its translation and issuance here, and essentially was simply and frankly a work in support of the author's country. The first, by Alfred Hoyt Granger (b. 1867), *England's World Empire*, was subtitled *Some Reflections Upon its Growth and Policy*, and was released by the influential Chicago publisher, Open Court, which was also the publisher of other books which made the banned list. Though offensive to Empire loyalists it became repelling to Americans by association, and like most of the list had a season when it circulated in America un-tainted by a "propaganda" tar-brush. But the study of this subject which really caught in British craws was Ernst graf zu Reventlow's *The Vampire of the Continent*. After understandably marked success in its German original at home, its appearance in New York in 1916 in an English language translation caused an additional stir. Under the imprint of the Jackson Press in New York City, it immediately became identified as part of the veritable library put out under the indefatigable German-American publicist, George Sylvester Viereck, about which more later. It was transparently a political book, a sustained attack on the role played by the British Empire in the affairs of mainland Europe. It is one of the two (out of the 47) publications which was to experience a readership to this day. It has had an off-and-on attraction to readers for the last two generations, and has surfaced once more in the late 1980s as a kind of cult book among connoisseurs of conspiratorial theories and their related literature. It certainly made sense 70 years ago to traditional exponents of Empire loyalty of the sort deriving from Clive, "Chinese" Gordon, Kipling, Cecil Rhodes, Kitchener and Churchill to keep Reventlow's thesis from as many American readers as possible.

The next two entries on the list, Frank Harris and Sven Hedin, were the two with the widest recognizability worldwide as writers and personalities of all the cited authors. Harris, 62 years old then, was one of the two "elder statesmen" of the list as well, enjoyed a very eminent reputation in the field of letters, a writer on many subjects, though considered scandalous by some for the boldness of his style and approach. Like many others he was electrified by the outbreak of the war in Europe in 1914, and soon after was in print on it. His *England or Germany?* — the title *did* end in a question mark, though the Army press release omitted it — had appeared in New York very quickly (Willmarth Press) and was already in its third printing in 1915, some 3-1/2 years before its belated addition to what Americans were not supposed to be reading. His detached attitude and Irish birth, though a naturalized U.S. citizen, may have helped out in the decision to target this work.

There are unresolved complications concerning Harris' book, however. Walter Millis in his famed study, *Road to War: America, 1914-1917* (Boston: Houghton Mifflin, 1935, pp. 202-203) declared that *England or Germany?* was one of "two of the most objective studies of America's relationship to the war published at that time" that he ever saw, referring to the first year of war in Europe. But Millis thought that the reputation of the work was flawed in effect because it later became known that Harris accepted money from the German Embassy representative, Dr. Albert (about whom more will be related when Bernhard Dernburg is discussed). Whether Harris agreed to write material sympathetic to the German cause or at least not hostile to it is not at issue here. However, Millis did not claim nor did anyone else at that time charge that *England or Germany?* had been under-written by German funds, though by the closing months of 1918 Allied counter-propagandists were casting a shadow of suspicion on nearly everything written at an earlier time, when it had been perfectly acceptable and matter-of-fact to do so. Millis was quite ambivalent on all this, however, Though ready to condemn the Germans for trying to find Americans to work for them in neutral days, he went on to say, "but where the Allies could command their thousands [*sic*] of devoted American propagandists, the Germans could command scarcely a handful." In view of the belated appendage of Harris' volume to the list of forbidden books on suspicion of its support, ostensibly, it was strange that New York University Professor Edwin J. Clapp's *Economic Aspects of the War: Neutral Rights, Belligerent Claims and American Commerce* (New Haven, Conn.: Yale University Press,

1915) did not also make the banned entries. Praised by Millis for its objectivity, it had been directly backed by German funds, though it might not have been generally known as such late in 1918.[16] (More will be said about the latter book and others with similar support subsequently.)

Sven Hedin, next listed after Harris, probably was even better known, worldwide. A celebrated Arctic explorer with wide acquaintance of other parts of the planet, his *With the German Armies in the West* was a large narrative written in a style which became even better known in later years, and it was decorated with no less than 119 illustrations. It was translated from its Swedish original to English, and, like Harris' book, was published also in 1915 (New York: John Lane Co.). Though it dealt almost exclusively with now-four-year-old military campaigns, someone thought that his mainly adventure narrative, intended primarily for young men readers in neutral Sweden in 1915, had something potentially sinister in it for someone now reading it in English in the U.S.A. late in 1918.

With Ernest F. Henderson, we are back with the professoriat in the department of potentially late-season subversiveness. A prolific writer on Germany for many years and also well after World War One (this writer had Henderson's *Short History of Germany* as assigned reading in a university history course in 1944), he had produced a brief work (only 97 pages) titled *Germany's Fighting Machine*, published late in 1914 by the major publisher Bobbs-Merrill. But this also seemed to contain a reprehensible and iniquitous message for someone, despite what he had concerned himself with being history for more than four years at that moment.

It was obvious from the next on the list, Frederic C. Howe (the list had his middle initial as "G"), that even profound supporters of the President were not immune. Howe was one of the country's best known local government students and vociferous reform critics for decades. His two pre-war books on the reorganization of city government and the pushing of municipal ownership had made him one of the best-known figures in the Progressive era, along with his championing of the People's Institute in New York. And his enthusiasm for the New Freedom characterized by the emergence of Woodrow Wilson evoked the most eloquent approval from Howe in the 1911-1914 days; one has to read his memoirs of the time in his subsequent book, *The Confessions of a Reformer* (1925). In fact, he essayed forth in an influential political job himself in 1914 as Commissioner of Immigration at the Port of New York, a job he held into 1919. He was in this post when his name on the Army book list surprised many; some had forgotten that he had written a semi-pacifist book of some size and impact, published by the major publisher Scribner in 1916, titled *Why War?* Intended at that time to supply what Howe and others of the old Progressive strain thought was a grave deficiency among the new political leadership, a dismal ignorance of world political realities, it probably was too late for this kind of education, and the swift joining of the belligerence forces by Mr. Wilson between the end of January and the beginning of April, 1917 was ample proof of that. But at the end of the summer of 1918, the eminence of Frederic C. Howe was not enough to erase from the record his publishing of a big book which has disparaged going to war, and directing attention to such within the country who wanted to do so. And so he joined the ranks of those charged with writing "German propaganda."

Following Howe on the list appeared to be a name out of place, but in proper context it appears that the error was one of transcription somewhere along the line. There was no war-era writer named "Roland Higgins." But — there was one named Roland *Hugins*. He was the author of the proscribed title *Germany Misjudged*. It would appear that the compilers of the Army list never read this, and had made up their minds after only spotting the title. They ignored the subtitle, *An Appeal to International Good Will in the Interest of a Lasting Peace*. Only 111 pages, it actually was not a continuous intellectual effort but rather a tome stitched together from previous magazine journalism, appearing first as articles in the magazine *Open Court* and then gathered together and published by the same auspices in 1916, with an introduction he had published in the New York *Times* in 1914, which mocked pro-British papers calling the Germans "monsters." Hugins, another remnant of the earlier strain in Progressivism, and an admirer and future biographer of former President Grover Cleveland, had views on the war very similar to those espoused by Mr. Wilson even as late as the end of January, 1917: a hope the war might be negotiated to an end without winners or losers via a tolerable settlement all around. But by now such sentiments had become support for the adversary.

Still another influential figure to make the list, the clerical inspirational speaker, Rufus M. Jones, did so via a simple 22-page pamphlet, a religious pacifist plea titled *A More Excellent Way* (New York: Association Press, 1916), also a catch of the late-season round-up. It was one of the few pamphlets present on the banned list, and presumably was one of the offending works found scattered about Army post libraries which provoked the alert by the War Library Service in the preliminary weeding-out process begun early in August, 1918.[17]

In addition to the sprinkling of mistakes in the names of authors and titles on the banned books list was a totally wrong attribution. *How to Protect Our Soldiers* was identified as the work of a Pacific Coast pamphleteer named William Samuel Leake, who seemed to be more interested in the contemporary national furor over Prohibition than the war. Actually the author was one Frederick Lawrence Rawson (b. 1859); his was a 135-page tract which also had seen the light of day prior to American belligerent status, a second edition having already been issued in 1917, which is apparently the one which attracted attention a year later. Rawson's title presumably excited suspicion that here was another effort to induce some kind of interference with the functioning of the armed forces, there already having been a number of incidents involving various aspects of this subject. But interest in it all apparently did not extend even beyond its main title, or it would have been discovered that the concern of the author was confined to a mystico-religious level, and emanating from a part of the country already establishing a reputation 70 years ago as a center for the incubation of exotica in the field of metaphysical and religious speculation. Subtitled *Or the Practical Utilization of the Power of God by Right Thinking*, it had been issued by the Metaphysical Library of Los Angeles. Like several strange entries on this strange list, what it was doing being identified as "German propaganda" was surely a test for the analytical and interpretative powers of our best intellects.

Despite the misconceptions about the above title, *How to Protect Our Soldiers,* it provokes additional speculations and ruminations which lead to related matters. If it be taken as genuine that the purpose of this offensive against books was the preservation and strengthening of the morale of the armed forces by seeking, at least on a general basis, protection from the enervating and sapping effect of reading experiences calculated to result from exposure to various kinds of views and ideas, such as material supposedly advocating the enemy's welfare and objectives, or religious and social views undermining official positions, it is obvious that the simple designation "German propaganda" was patently insufficient. In this event, there were other categories of reading which should have been watched for and condemned as well. One that was totally ignored consisted of accounts of the dark side of martial combat, especially in this war, in which the dead and wounded reached totals sometimes in the six figures in a single week, something completely incomprehensible 70 years later, when casualties are counted in handfuls over periods of a fortnight. (In the battle of the Somme beginning July 1, 1916 the British lost 60,000 men *on one day*, the approximate loss of the U.S. armed forces in Vietnam in over *twelve years*.)

And what of those whose job it was to patch together the multitudes grievously injured in all this? No studies or narratives of this side of war made the list of prohibited reading posted by the Army, even such a profoundly depressing work as Ellen N. LaMotte's *Backwash of War* (New York: Putnam, 1916). This volunteer American nurse's account of what she experienced in the hospitals and field dressing stations in the early period of the war before American involvement ranked up there with the war's goriest narratives, probably unbeatable for description of sheer horror. And it had been around for two years by the time the Army tally sheet was proclaimed. Probably no other book approached this one for its potential influence upon the young and impressionable, presumably a fair fraction of those expected to engage an enemy in Europe, in a war which was expected to last for years beyond 1918. But this title and the entire class of literature it represented failed to register a single item in the list which the Army thought its soldiers should not be reading.

It may be that those most concerned with the psychological underpinning of American soldiery considered insulating them from such books as LaMotte's unnecessary because of the spread and popularity of tomes by people who downplayed the trench-warfare gore, the grotesque, outlandish high-explosive mutilations, the windrows of the machine-gunned, the amputations, the mustard gas burns and the shell-shock to the point of vanishing, and buoyed popular spirits with inspirational messages, gravely censored the tales of combat, and spread high-flying abstractions which diverted most from reality, a war which was turned into a bloodbath that made an abattoir an insignificance by comparison. A prime example of the literature which steered the populace into the realms of illusionary glory was *Over the Top* (New York: Putnam, 1917), by Arthur Guy Empey, an American volunteer who fought in combat with the British for the better part of the first two years of the war until invalided out of the British armed services by wounds, and whose literary contribution based on this experience was being read long after the end of hostilities. It was the better part of a decade before books like LaMotte's began to get substantive competition, even though disillusionist tracts started almost with the final stilling of the guns. (The German analog to Empey appeared after the war [1922] and in English translation by Basil Creighton as *Storm of Steel* [New York: Doubleday, Doran, 1929]. It outmatched Empey in glorying in the worst aspects of combat, while establishing its author, Ernst Juenger, as a name in the writing of war books, a field in which he was to score with a dozen works issued in several countries. Wounded 14 times in the first three years of the war, Juenger was spared what befell millions of his countrymen, some of the most ghastly fates being reproduced in German pictorial collections in the '20s. The excerpts compiled by Frederick A. Barber published in New York in 1932 as *The Horror Of It* [Harcourt] have been cited repeatedly as comprising the most grisly gallery of war photographs ever published in the English-speaking world. An interesting and rewarding intellectual exercise would be a scanning of the Barber anthology while reading carefully C.R.M.F. Cruttwell's epic *History of the Great War,* published by Oxford in 1934, and still in a class by itself as a one-volume account of the war of 1914-1918.)

Of the more than two score writers of the books denounced by the Secretary of the Army as deleterious to the intellectual and morale health of the U.S.A.'s conscript army in the late summer of 1918, hardly a half-dozen were what might be described generally as those with national reputations, of whatever kind. The most notorious by some margin, however, was not the consequence of prolific production as one might have noted in the case of Dr. David Starr Jordan, George Sylvester Viereck, or Professor Scott Nearing. It grew from a career of sensational publicity. This was the case of I.T.T. Lincoln, whose varied exploits and involvements in the first third of the 20th century approximated the real life equivalent of that of the picaresque rogue "hero" of de Lizárdi's epic novel, *The Itching Parrot.*

Lincoln, identified by the anonymous reviewer of his book *Revelations of An International Spy* in *The Nation* ("Every Man His Own Spy," January 27, 1916, pp. 94-95) as "the young Hungarian Jew who first came to London at about the age of twenty" (born in 1879, this must have been at the turn of the century), had already had a succession of experiences that might have excited the imaginative talents of a minor-league Rabelais or Cervantes. A Member of Parliament at 30, variously thereafter an itinerant missionary in Canada, an Anglican curate in Kent, in southeast England, and then private secretary to a big English cocoa manufacturer, he seems to have found time for journalistic enterprise and a claimed involvement as a pre-war spy, ostensibly for Imperial Germany, in at least three countries.

Somehow he had managed to get back to North America once more, this time to the United States. Several months before the publication of his book by the established firm of McBride, Nast & Co., he was arrested by American authorities in Brooklyn on August 4, 1915 at the complaint of the British consul in New York on charges of forgery and theft in Britain, which had been lodged there two months earlier. The charges were repeated by the British Ambassador to the U.S.A., Sir Cecil Spring-Rice, who had relayed the complaint to his consular subordinate, and to whom New York and federal police responded, since there were no outstanding charges against Lincoln in the United States. (New York *Times,* August 5, 1915, p. 1.)

Lincoln (his initials stood for "Ignatius Timothy Trebich," though another source had called him "Isaac Nebitsch") had claimed to be a spy for Imperial Germany some time before his arrest, and reiterated this upon his apprehension by the police, while denying the other charges. But the British complaint simply charged him with forgery and misappropriation of funds related to an oil business purportedly based in Rumania, involving the use of an Englishman's name in a financial transaction related to this venture, which allegedly had defrauded English and American investors of several hundred thousand dollars. This made him liable to extradition according to the terms of the extant British-American treaty; a charge of espionage would not. Lincoln was lodged in the Raymond Street jail in Brooklyn for over five months, frequently out on escorted trips to the Federal Building not far away, for repeated interrogations and providing translations of papers in the German language in which the Department of Justice was interested. In the meantime a series of legal maneuvers was taking place, postponing action on the extradition request from London.

On Saturday afternoon, January 15, 1916 Lincoln escaped from a deputy U.S. Marshal in whose custody he happened to be. A many-sided scandal evolved from this, and three different police forces were soon searching for him (New York *Times,* January 19, 1916, p. 2). For weeks the entire matter approached a comic act, with Lincoln, who apparently never left the New York area, leaving messages at the offices of an afternoon newspaper, the New York *American,* while also making a series of telephone calls there, and to his publisher, McBride, Nast, located at 31 East 17th Street in Manhattan.

Six days after his escape from police custody his book was published. (New York *Times,* January 23, 1916, Sec. II, p. 5.) It began to appear that his spectacular caper had been long planned, and undertaken to provide sensational publicity for his book. McBride, Nast admitted having several conversations with him after his escape, and also that he had told them even before then that he had planned to do so. Five days after publishing his *Revelations,* McBride, Nast issued a statement calling for public support for Lincoln, and alleging that he could not get a fair trial in England, following revelation of a letter received from him. (New York *Times,* January 21, 1916, p. 2; January 27, 1916, p. 2.)

In the meantime Lincoln was still trading on his claims to being a spy, while officials both in London and New York were scoffing at all this, making sure that the understanding was established that no effort would be made whatever to prosecute him for espionage. An official of the Bureau of Investigation declared bluntly that Lincoln "had never done anything" for the U.S.A., and that he had never been given access to any document "to which we attached any value," while the Assistant Superintendent at the Bureau, Joseph A. Baker, denied there was a scrap of evidence in their possession that Lincoln had ever been a spy for anyone (see issue of the *Times* for January 27, 1916, above). A short time later it was admitted that Lincoln was receiving money from New York area Germans, and that they had hired legal counsel for him. Scotland Yard deflated his claim to be knowledgeable of German government ciphers, an inspector for the Yard declaring they had given him a German enciphered dispatch, and that he had failed to make out anything of it at all (New York *Times,* January 20, 1916, p. 2). (Lincoln apparently played both sides according to his advantage; the British belatedly circulated in the U.S.A. a campaign document of Lincoln's when he was trying to get elected as a Liberal candidate for Parliament in 1910. While extolling British society he denigrated that of Germany, alleging that the situation was so bad there that the populace had been reduced to eating horse and dog meat.)

Lincoln remained at large for 35 days. He was re-arrested on Broadway in Manhattan on February 19, 1916 and returned to the Brooklyn jail he had fled. It was at this time that the New York *Times* revealed that the family name was Schlesinger, and that the notorious adventurer had a brother named Joseph living in Manhattan, but who refused to talk to *Times* reporters about the entire affair. (New York *Times,* February 20, 1916, Sec. I, p. 1; February 21, 1916, p. 3.)

The spring of 1916 was spent in a succession of appeals to an order for extradition, which eventually went to the level of the Supreme Court. Upon exhaustion of this avenue, the lower court's order was sustained. Two Scotland Yard inspectors took custody of him on May 26, upon his delivery to the British liner *Cameronia,* and they sailed the next day. (New York *Times,* May 27, 1916, p. 6; May 28, 1916, p. 5.) Arraigned in London on June 13, he was tried and found guilty "almost immediately" by a jury on two counts of forgery on July 4 and received concurrent sentences of three years on each; his book *Revelations of an International Spy* had been in print by now almost six months. (New York *Times,* July 5, 1916, p. 5.) One could not say that British justice worked slowly in this case; one can hardly imagine anything propelled so expeditiously, probably aggravated by all the attention the matter had received, not so much by the amount of money involved. Undoubtedly Lincoln's self-esteem was bruised by the British disdain for his claims of being a spy,[18] which in turn reflected unfavorably upon his book, its contents, and his publisher. It was in truth very difficult to determine if he had ever found out anything of use whatsoever to the German government. And there were fewer to take him seriously anyway, despite the entertaining nature of the yarns in his 322-page work.

What is somewhat more puzzling is why his tome ended up on Secretary Baker's forbidden list over two years later, by which time it had received wide circulation. In fact, considering the widespread periodical comment, some of it by Lincoln himself, and in view of the swirl of attention already achieved by the author, and the linage he had already received in American papers, as well as gossip, it was the one title of all the 47 which it might be assumed an American interested in adventure and intrigue might already have read. Again, it may be that British intelligence was most put out by Lincoln's book on the basis of some of its assertions unrelated to the melodramatic parts of its contents, a possible reason why it made this American roll of dishonor, so to speak. One claim in the book had got under a few skins early in its promotion, an assertion by Lincoln that a calculated program of Germanophobia had been deliberately instigated in Britain in mass communications in the pre-war years of the early 20th century, including the declaration that Sir Valentine Chirol, foreign editor of the London *Times,* had made it incumbent on all its Continental correspondents "to suppress everything that might have a beneficial influence or effect on Anglo-German relations."[19]

Among the interdicted authors being examined and analyzed were five women, one of whom has been discussed. Two others may be taken together here, though on separate lists, since their product was substantially of the same order. On the first list was Mary Ethel Macauley (the list misspelled her last name), whose substantial book *Germany in War Time: What An American Girl Saw and Heard* was published by Open Court in Chicago in 1917. On the second list was the much-published journalist, Madeleine Zabriskie Doty. Though only authors were on this second posting, not titles, at least as it involved the press release, it must be assumed the objectionable work was the latter's *Short Rations: An American Woman in Germany, 1915-1916,* issued in New York by the major house of Century, also in 1917. Again it was a case of belated recognition of "German propaganda," both writers testifying to the humanity of the enemy without expressing a proper degree of hostility and loathing which the new conditions called for. But again it was a case of observers commenting on experiences during a time when their American homeland was not a war participant. (Doty's book was based on two visits to Germany, the second in 1916.)

Adhering to this topical format once more, we may take up the most irrelevant and surely one of the most explosive subjects dealt with in this strange spread of outlawed material, the authors and titles dealing with Ireland. Again we are faced with mystery if we keep in mind the basic Government position that the titles on its list were "German propaganda." The three books involved here were unabashedly *Irish* propaganda, but their relationship to advancing German views on anything unrelated to the future of Ireland cannot be sustained. The main angle pertinent to the war was the suspicion or apprehension on the part of the British that Imperial Germany would exploit the touchy situation with assistance to the Irish, and this charge was widely made by many British spokesmen, just as heatedly denied by some Irish partisans. It surely had a critical part to play in the banning of the book by James K. McGuire, *What Could Germany Do For Ireland?*, issued in New York by the Wolf Tone Company in the rebellion year of 1916 (only an Irishman could appreciate the significance of the name of the publishing front responsible for McGuire's book.) Undoubtedly there were Irish both in Ireland and elsewhere in the world who thought for a time that Germany would open a new war front in Ireland, which would have had a profound effect on the course of the war on mainland Europe. It is incontrovertible that books such as McGuire's and those by Margaret Skinnider, *Doing My Bit For Ireland* (New York: Century, 1917) and Seumas MacManus, *Ireland's Case,* already in a third edition (New York: Irish Publishing Co., 1918), were grave aggravations to the British and their hope of keeping Ireland in its ancient political relationship to Britain, but again what they did for "German propaganda" requires exquisite word-shaving on the part of investigators. MacManus was already a famed homeland figure in Irish literature but few realized that McGuire was a former mayor of the city of Syracuse, New York. And he had anticipated this whole business with a book even more provoking than his suppressed title, *King, the Kaiser and Irish Freedom* which the New York house specializing in Irish books, Devin-Adair, had brought out in 1915, and which the new censors completely overlooked. (The mercurial political situation in Ireland, 1914-1918 and after, is discussed succinctly by MacManus in his very successful book *The Story of the Irish Race,* first published in 1921, and with innumerable editions and printings since; on the Irish rebellion of April 24-29, 1916 his chapter 79 in printings since 1944 is probably the best on the subject for the space devoted to it. In subsequent listing of the books by MacManus in later years, it was noted that *Ireland's Case* was generally omitted.)

Less than a fifth of the people involved in an action which professed to be motivated solely by "German propaganda" turned out to be Germans of any kind. Two were German nationals whose work was not originally directed to an American audience, while four were German-Americans, who at least until the U.S.A. became involved in the war had as much right to be writing kind things in the interests of their ancestral home as did the legions of people of British derivation who were similarly engaged, in America. In a sixth case the concern was over publications by a man two years deceased at the time the denunciation of his work began, while in an important but separate operation, the book of a seventh was impounded by the Justice Department rather than the Army Library people, as will be seen in a separate context. Standing out, as usual, was the capricious and unsystematic approach used in selecting the authors and their works for suppression, the irrelevance of some if not all and the unexplained neglect of virtually every title known to be subsidized by German money and frankly and deliberately intended to perform a German propaganda role. It was almost as though those in charge had been "programmed" to do the reverse of what was originally devised and planned, to use a modern expression.

An index to the ill-conceived nature of the Army assault on enemy propaganda was to be seen in the very first targeted title by someone with a German name, which appeared on the list-of-five early in August, 1918, to be appended to the somewhat larger one three weeks later. *What Germany Wants* by Edmund von Mach sounded to someone as though it were an official pronouncement by the Imperial German Foreign Office, apparently. But this brief (157 pages) treatise was somewhat more speculative than "official," and was the work of a German-American. Furthermore, it was not a labor surreptitiously distributed from a covert basement press operation, but, at the time of suppression, had been in circulation for four calendar years in the U.S.A. under the auspices of one of the two most prestigious publishing operations in Boston, the Little, Brown Company. Characteristically, all the rest of von Mach's output was utterly ignored.[20]

The obtuseness continued with the exorcising of one more work dating back to 1914, Professor Hugo Muensterberg's *The War and America* (the list had substituted "in" for "and" in the title), one of his almost annual stream of books, this one issued by the major house of Appleton in New York, and the German national Hellmuth von Muecke's *The Emden* (the list left off the article in this title). Muensterberg had been brought from Germany to become part of the faculty at Harvard College, and was one of its major intellectual lights. Deceased since 1916, it was rather late in the season to detect something sinister about his product, though he had been increasingly criticized for his frank support of his mother country. Von Muecke's book, which had wide circulation in Germany, was actually one of four he had written about the famed German warship and its landing party, a raider of British commerce in the Indian Ocean and elsewhere in the early months of the war until hunted down and destroyed by units of the British fleet. This was a war adventure story, not "propaganda," and its availability from the Boston-based specialist in German books, Ritter and Company, since 1917, was hardly circumspect.

In the case of Frederick F. Schrader's *German-American Handbook,* a self-published work sold from the author's home in New York City, we had here another labor by a German-American which probably came under the heading of sentimental antiquarianism. Schrader had attempted to supply a type of "heritage" encyclopedia reminding Americans of German ancestry of their cultural roots, not trying to denounce those of anyone else. Though America proliferated with clubs, societies, educational fronts, linguistic study groups and heirloom galleries as well as other institutions reminding Americans of descent from the British Isles, France and other European lands of their forebears and ethnic inheritance, when the Germans did this, their efforts had the twisted taint of "hyphenate" attached to them. By now in late 1918 Germanophobia had become psychopathic, and such works as Schrader's (issued in 1916) were open-season, in a war climate which no longer concerned a political clash over the disposition of Europe, but had become in many minds an extermination process applying to even the faintest strain of Teutonic culture, thanks in large part to the exploitation of an outrageously promoted campaign of fabricated atrocity propaganda.

And bringing up the rear in the futile and obviously ineffective attack on books by persons of German ancestry as carriers of dread "propaganda" disease was the most ridiculous of all, the citing of a tiny anthology of poetry by George Sylvester Viereck. If there was one entry in the entire bibliography which typified the ignorance behind the entire project, it was this 60-page *Songs of Armageddon and Other Poems,* published in New York by Mitchell Kennerly in 1916. It might have been compared to a disarming of an enemy in which he had been deprived of his crossbow and arquebus, but allowed to keep his machine guns, heavy artillery and bombing planes. If there was one continuous beehive of German propaganda production in the country down into 1917 it was that taking place under the multifarious operations supervised by Viereck, publisher of the famed journal *The Fatherland,* and an assiduous supporter of getting a stream of books into print under either his own sponsorship or financed by others.[21] It is not the task of this study to examine the vast subject of propaganda in World War One but simply to analyze the subject as it concerned the Army's venture into its suppression in the closing weeks of the war. But the preposterousness of banning Viereck's slight booklet of verse while ignoring totally all the rest of the library he had sponsored and was responsible for lent a broad aspect of the comic to the total enterprise.[22] In the case of the remaining undiscussed German, Bernhard Dernburg, an actual official of Imperial Germany based in the U.S.A. for about nine months, 1914-1915, the ramifications and consequences of his stay here and presence eventually on the banned book list will be taken up in relation to the September, 1918 amendment.

The presence of Professor Scott Nearing on the Secretary of War's forbidden reading quarantine indicated still another strain of American thinking hostile or considered "alien" to the "war effort," though one which hardly was alien or "subversive" in a strictly American sense if one were mindful of history. Professor Nearing represented a vein of socialist thinking which was simply opposed to the war in principle, while proposing specific reasons for thinking like that. Similar sensibilities were widely shared in the U.S.A. The Midwest and High Plains states especially crawled with critics and protesters who shared little if anything with imported radicalism, and who sounded like Nearing all the time, a tendency which stretched from the Post- Civil War Greenbackers to the days of Huey Long.

Nearing struck deep traditional roots with his criticism of the economic consequences of the war buildup prior to entry into the war, and on an increasingly strident basis after involvement. With "dollar patriotism" at its peak, writing such as Nearing's was bound to be regarded as the height of scurrility by elements prospering from it all, late in 1918.[23] But in view of the continuous investigations scattered through the next 20 years of outrageous "profiteering" on war contracts, and on some occasions revelations that billions of taxpayer's dollars were squirreled away by people who produced little if anything in the form of production for the prosecution of the war,[24] it would seem that Nearing deserved at least a tentative audience and not suppression. (Actually, criticism of this aspect of the war grew so voluble during hostilities that reference works frankly introduced the word "profiteering" as a section under which titles of articles so concerned were grouped for easy consultation; the subject excited so much talk and print that even the President engaged in decrying "profiteering" on occasion, publicly.)

Nearing, for an academic personality, operated in dramatic ways. Just 35 years old, at the time of the stir over the books, he was already the author of eight major books on various economic and sociological themes, as well as several other works. He had already been dismissed from one teaching post (ultimately, two), that from the University of Pennsylvania in 1915 resulting in a nation-wide controversy which boiled in the papers and magazines for years. But what aroused the most resentment was his scathing pamphlets criticizing the management and direction of what were known as the war industries, as well as the conduct of the war itself, on economic grounds. One might comment, though, that the War Department had slighted him in citing just one work, when a veritable one-man list might have been promulgated consisting of just his productions of the same order. And the scope of his activities did not slow him down, as he was to produce a dozen publications during the war and its immediate aftermath.

It would appear that the listing for Professor Nearing on Secretary Baker's second list was a generic title. It was known that he had written two "open letters" to the New York *Times* on the general subject of wartime profiteering on the part of military suppliers of various kinds. But the *Times* called no attention to them, and evidence was not found that any publication of the two together ever took place. This of course was just part of the situation. Professor Nearing was an established formidable opponent of the war drive well before the *Times* letters, and an indefatigable pamphleteer in this cause before and after the U.S. war declaration. His participation in the Rip-Saw series, issued out of St. Louis (National Rip-Saw Publications, based at 411 Olive Street) was famed, and their No. 24 by Nearing, *Germs of War: A Study in Preparedness,* was found especially aggravating by the exponents of the pro-war drive.

About ten weeks after formal American belligerence there came into existence a broad political front named the Peoples Council of America (New York *Times,* June 21, 1917, p. 3), and Professor Nearing became the chairman of its executive committee three months later (New York *Times,* September 18, 1917, p. 4). Five weeks after that the PCA, already daily badgered as a "pro-German" organization, which it daily denied, printed as its *Bulletin* for October 24 Nearing's work now titled *Huge Red War Profits: A Second Open Letter to the New York Times*; the first could not be found. It is very likely that this edition was expected to be suppressed and confiscated (it sold for two cents), and may have been one of the things found lying around here and there in Army camp libraries.

Why just his provocative critiques of "profiteering" addressed to the *Times* should have made the Army's list was a puzzler. It seemed to some that they could at least have also added the pamphlet, also published in 1917, which got Professor Nearing indicted under the Espionage Act six months before, *The Great Madness: A Victory for the American Plutocracy* (New York *Times,* March 22, 1918, p. 4). The implication again was that all the other provocative things Professor Nearing had published were perfectly permissible for the men in the U.S. Army to read.[25]

Professor Nearing remained in the home front wartime political trenches, even running for office in the national congressional election in the first week of November, 1918 as the Socialist Party candidate for the House of Representatives seat from New York held by Fiorello H. LaGuardia, then in the armed services in the branch which was the ancestor of the Army Air Corps, and stationed in Italy apparently on some political mission. Major LaGuardia was already under fire from constituents who called on him to resign from the Army and resume his political duties or face a recall. The war government re-routed him back to the U.S.A. where he campaigned against Nearing for a short time and was re-elected, the event calling him to national attention which led to his generation-long career especially in national and New York state politics.[26] (Nearing's platform, formulated well before November 1918, called for an immediate negotiation of the end of the European war. That it did come to a halt less than a week after the election might have been construed by his partisans as a political "victory" of sorts, even if achieved in an obviously indirect manner, and a product of a different political enterprise than Nearing had envisioned.)

To round out a list of literary products which in the main must have been the despair of German propaganda hunters was the religious mystico-pacific treatise by Theodora Wilson Wilson, *The Last Weapon,* an essay of 188 pages which had already gone through *six* editions by December 1916 in simultaneous publication in both England and the U.S.A. (C.W. Daniel Ltd. and Winston, respectively).

The author, a well known novelist and playwright with a career spanning the first four decades of the 20th century, had apparently with this work prepared something with a very slow fuse to be around this long before exciting someone's attention, though this may have come about as a result of a seventh appearance in the U.S.A. in 1917.[27] (Ignored in the process was her *The Weapon Unsheathed: A Spiritual Adventure,* which Daniel also brought out in 1916, but which presumably escaped citation because it appeared to be confined to circulation in Britain.)

When Secretary Baker's office released the information covering the final 16 works under the Army library sanction on September 25, the news story was somewhat abridged. Only seven authors and only one title were mentioned by name, and the news was buried deeply in the back pages of the newspapers if mentioned at all. This amended list got far less attention and in several instances aroused no action at all before the end of the war. But the writers who were identified were almost all well known, compared to most of those decorating the original list, and deserve extended attention in view of their prominence at one time or another. But only in one or two cases was it possible to speculate fairly correctly as to what they had written which the Army censors and their assistants had found offensive.

Easily the most prominent of the final list of those accused of creating German propaganda was David Starr Jordan, an eminent biologist, President or Chancellor of Stanford University for a quarter of a century (1891-1916) and a national figure through involvement in many public affairs (Dr. Jordan was published over 70 times in the periodical press alone during the war years). He had excited great controversy with a lengthy series of addresses in several U.S. cities between the breaking of diplomatic relations with Germany in February, 1917 and the declaration of war two months later, arguing vehemently against getting involved in the war. Later, he had changed tunes, following April 6, and spoke in behalf of supporting the war, as he related in his memoirs of the time, *The Days of a Man* (1922). But this later support apparently had not washed out remembrance of what he had done prior to formal belligerence. As one of the academic world's most prolific writers (it is doubtful if he has ever had an equal among administrators of American higher education) he undoubtedly authored something to aggravate the ideological watch-men patrolling the American ideological scene during the April, 1917-September, 1918 period. But the news release did not identify the title of the offending work.

Jordan's considerable reputation as a biologist had led him into related areas involving war and statecraft which actually spun off in other directions from his interest in peace as a national policy. Despite his vociferous activity in the anti-involvement agitation of 1915-1917 his main concern appeared to be his conviction leading from his biological studies that war was dramatically dysgenic, and increasingly so in the form of mass combat from Napoleonic times onward. It was not a position likely to gladden the heart of military or political leaders in the mega-death days of World War One, with its six-figure battle death totals in single weeks of a succession of cam-paigns, though most of Jordan's written product in support of his the-sis had been published well before American entry into the war. Of particular importance here included *Blood of a Nation: A Study of the Decay of Races Through the Survival of the Unfit* (San Francisco: A. Carlisle & Co., 1912); *War's Aftermath* (Boston: Houghton, 1914), frankly labeled "a study of the eugenics of war," and devoted to an examination of "racial or biological consequences" of the American Civil War in three counties in the South; "Our Blighted Race," an article in the *Journal of Education* in 1915, and a substantial study published by the American Unitarian Association in Boston in the same year, *War and the Breed: The Relation of War to the Downfall of Nations.*

[Two world wars have come close to killing Europe. No part of the world can engage in the destruction of so many millions of its healthiest and most intelligent men, and pretend to be better for it as a result, no matter how loud is its tiresome palaver about having eradi-cated Political Sin while so occupied. That the latter has been a lie of galactic proportions may be beside the point, as blather of this kind is simply a cosmetic disguise for what wars within the confrontational-adversarial State system are fought for and about. It is enough to point out that, in view of the vast grave that Europe has become, even if it never divides and fights among itself again, it will have a prodi-gious struggle on its hands in the next century if it hopes to escape becoming the planet's first Fourth World. David Starr Jordan could have produced a five-foot-shelf of volumes, had he been young enough to survive two decades past the end of World War Two, on the galloping degeneracy he could have observed, described and evaluated while seated in the debris of 1939-1945.

As it was, Dr. Jordan created enough of a stir with *War and the Breed*. Finished in the spring of 1915, it had a stark, morose message, describing the outlandish dysgenic results of war over the years among the peoples of Europe. It ended with a substantial survey of various aspects of the war then going on, with its stunning inroads among the males of the peoples at war, without digressing into a discussion as to how it had all come about. His special attention to the decimation taking place among the best British types, killed in action, 1914-1915, and childless as well, must have seriously aggravated the pace-setters of opinion-making in the British war party, who of course could do nothing about its distribution in the U.S.A. for over two years before American belligerency. It surely deserved a top rating among books to be extirpated from American armed forces libraries after mid-summer, 1917, but unexplainably was not even alluded to in Secretary Baker's first list over a year later. Curiously enough, an abridged edition of this book has been published by the Cliveden Press of Washington, D.C. in the summer of 1988.]

The deceased Professor Muensterberg enjoyed the distinction of being the only person who was cited on two of the forbidden book lists, appearing on this one but with no attention called publicly to the particular title. It was the suspicion, however, that the item this time was one of Professor Muensterberg's very last writings, *Tomorrow: Letters to a Friend in Germany,* a 274-page tome published by Appleton in 1916.

In addition to Madeleine Zabriskie Doty there were two distinguished male journalists also cited in the second list (actually, the third), Edward Lyell Fox and J. O'Donnell Bennett. The latter became celebrated at the very start of the war, and the ramifications and consequences of what ensued in his case deserve extended attention. To be cited late in 1918 suggested that someone had a long memory in his case as well, as one might not expect that more than a few might be able to recall that Bennett was one of the foreign correspondents accompanying the German armed forces forces in the first few weeks of the war in the West in August, 1914, in which party were also such well known journalists as Irvin S. Cobb, Harry Hansen, John T. McCutcheon and Roger Lewis. In Belgium in September, 1914 they had come across an accumulation of newspapers which they had not previously seen which purported to describe many atrocities allegedly committed by German troops. Outraged and appalled by what they considered to be flat-out fabrications, they had jointly sent off to the Associated Press in New York a cabled denunciation of these tales as groundless, a position fully backed by investigations later conducted in the area of hostilities by an attaché of the U.S. Embassy in Paris, apparently unofficially. This was of no avail, as the drumbeat of atrocity stories increased and ultimately became an unceasing cacophony through most of the war, and still is believed in the main almost 75 years later in large parts of the world. The prohibited work by Bennett may have been his formal presentation of his protest over these inventive yearns in a booklet, *Open Letter to Sir Arthur [Conan] Doyle,* published in Chicago at the end of 1914. (Sir Arthur was not only the creator of Sherlock Holmes; he was also the creator of some of the most innovative atrocity propaganda helping to inflame readers of English in the "Allied" populations, in the war of 1914-1918. But he had assistance in this enterprise from other noted British literary figures of some numbers, and probably never topped the declaration of the equally famed Rudyard Kipling, when the latter announced in the London *Morning Post* for June 22, 1915: "there are only two divisions in the world today — humans and Germans." Quoted by E.D. Morel, *Truth and the War,* third ed., 1918, p. 207; see note 32.) American fans and enthusiasts of Conan Doyle's famed mystery stories have not been known to pay marked attention to him as a historian, or even know of or acknowledge his talent in this department. But the major New York publisher Doran did issue in 1916 and 1917 his two-volume, over-600-page *History of the Great War,* an account of the first two years of the European combat, which reviewers noted was largely devoted to accounts of British bravery and heroic performance.

The recruiting of distinguished literary personalities to produce or front for war propaganda works, atrocity or otherwise, was one of the strokes of genius demonstrated by the British war government. No other participant in the war of 1914-1918 came close to their achievements in this regard. Working with the renowned elders were energetic up-and-coming younger men, where their first substantial experience was gained. Undoubtedly the most influential labor of this sort was the notorious Bryce Report (*Report of the Committee on Alleged German Outrages* [London, 1915]), chaired by the elder statesman of British political scholarship, James, Viscount Bryce (1838-1922). Purporting to document mass German atrocities committed in Belgium in the early months of the war, it was only 60 pages long, but had a 300-page appendix which presumably contained the "proof," citations drawn from 300 of 1,200 depositions made by Belgians in Britain, entirely unsworn statements made under uncontrolled conditions by people who provoked one exasperated British judge to remark that the "scum" of Belgium had seemingly descended upon his country.

The Bryce Report carried much weight in the U.S.A. because Viscount Bryce was well known there, had long before published a vast and acclaimed study of the American political system (*The American Commonwealth,* 2 vols., 1888) and had been British Ambassador to the U.S. from 1907 to 1913. The fate of the Report however was to be irretrievably tattered. A Belgian government report in 1922 failed to substantiate a single item in this catalog of atrocity charges and ultimately the entire collection of 1,200 depositions disappeared from British archives; scholarly researchers for the 20 years after the war failed to uncover a single one.

Nevertheless, this sensational production did its work, and paved the way for still another atrocity report fronted by Viscount Bryce, this one against the ally of Germany, the Turks, of even more appalling accusations of actions taken against the Armenian minority in their country (though little was said if anything about Armenian assistance to the enemies of Turkey which had something to do with it all). This second Bryce Report, *The Treatment of Armenians in the Ottoman Empire, 1915-1916* (London, 1916), was largely the work of a young British scholar, barely 26 years of age, Arnold J. Toynbee (1889-1975), but who was destined in the last 35 years of his life to become the veritable apex of British Establishment historical reputation. Entrusted by Viscount Bryce to edit the entire work, Toynbee apparently failed to question a single one of the 150 documents on which the report was based, and presented what was described in the publication's foreword as "one long catalog of horrors for which hardly any parallel can be found either in ancient or modern history"; Turks have been trying to modify the effects of this Toynbeean achievement without success for over 70 years. (Ignored from then to now was the caution at that time in the same foreword by Gilbert Murray, Regius Professor of Greek at Oxford, of the tendency and propensity of "oriental races"for the use of "hyperbolical language.")

Neglected by students of World War One propaganda also from then to now was Toynbee's part in recycling the substance of the first Bryce Report in the U.S. after American belligerence became an official act. His *German Terror in Belgium: An Historical Record,* was issued here by the publisher Doran almost in tandem with their publication of Conan Doyle's second volume (see above), in 1917, and reviewed with almost hysterical agreement in many major American newspapers and magazines in the first nine months of American involvement. The result was the citation of the Bryce Report of 1915 by Americans in published works for many years, long after it had been discredited and abandoned overseas.

The famed Western Union wire from the foreign correspondents to the Associated Press and their newspapers dated September 3, 1914 appeared very shortly after in a pro-German volume by a German-American, Rudolph Cronau, *British Black Book,* but relatively few Americans saw it in that source, a self-published work, despite six editions from 1914 to 1917. In view of the suppression and confiscation of this book by the Justice Department shortly after American entry into the war, using the Espionage Act as their authority, it was well after the end of the war before there was general awareness of this event, by which time it did not matter, as belief in German "atrocities" was deeply entrenched, and it no longer was of pressing interest.[28] The publication of the full wire in *Papers Relating to the Foreign Relations of the United States* (Washington, D.C., 1928), pp. 801-802, was followed by its re-publication in Lord Arthur Ponsonby's *Falsehood in Wartime* (New York: Dutton, 1928), p. 130, and in C. Hartley Grattan's *Why We Fought*[29] (New York: Vanguard, 1929),

p. 72.

This remarkable incident has bearing in additional impact upon the subject at hand in that it brings up the matter of prior intervention in the reading of Americans well before belligerence on the part of the Wilson Government. The era of "neutrality" did not prevent continuous *sub-rosa* meddling in the field of literature, mainly in behalf of pro-British partisans as well as the effort to keep American reading matter as one-sided as possible. Professor James Morgan Read, in his extremely useful and durable book, *Atrocity Propaganda, 1914-1919* (Yale University Press, 1941), pointed out that there was very little atrocity propaganda by Germans circulated outside Germany itself. In North America this was virtually a monopoly of the French, British and Belgians, so it was easy for people to conclude that charges of this sort came only from one side because it was only their adversaries who were committing these outrages.[30]

This widely disseminated protest by American writers on the groundless basis of the accusations which came to their attention at the end of August, 1914 was one of the few times that any balance at all was achieved during the war in America on this subject (Professor Read's study, published much later, concluded that the vast majority of atrocity stories throughout the war were baseless or unsubstantiated and that there was precious little support for or verification of any of these sensational yarns by any testimony taken after the war when the "witnesses" were under oath). The Cronau *British Black Book* in one sense was one of the few books issued in the U.S.A. which even peripherally grazed the atrocities issue from the German point of view. But there was this aspect of covert intelligence concerning what was reaching an American reading public which introduces a complication to the subject of the Army Department action in August-September, 1918.

Suspicion that various works were "German-financed" well predated the events which are the topic of this study, and what Grattan called "American government snoopers" had made at least one compilation of such suspected literature, and maybe more than one, well before U.S. belligerence. On page 91 of *Why We Fought*, Grattan published a list of ten such books, three of which (as noted by asterisks below) were later on the Army's list of forbidden tomes proscribed near the end of the war. They have been reorganized in alphabetical order from that source as follows:[31]

> J.W. Burgess — *America's Relation to the Great War**
> J.H. Labberton — *Belgium and Germany: A Dutch View*
> Ludwig Lewisohn — *The Spirit of Modern German Literature*
> Edmund von Mach — *What Germany Wants**
> Hugo Muensterberg — *The Americans**
> Frederick Naumann — *Central Europe*
> Francis Neilson — *How Diplomats Make War*[32]
> Bertrand Russell — *Justice in War Time*
> Ferdinand Schevill — *The Making of Modern Germany*
> Israel Zangwill — *The War for a World*

The entire story of the pursuit and later suppression of books and pamphlets by the Wilson Government well before the period April, 1917 through November, 1918 and maybe after it is not our subject, though a few incidents have been introduced here and there to indicate that it was a possibly substantial affair. Though Grattan concluded that "government agents succeeded in finding out practically nothing at all about what books were German financed" (pp. 91-92), including all ten of the above titles, one can see that the net was cast far and wide, though seining only a minnow or two, while managing to miss even the few substantial fish that later investigation and study located. And the strange part of this is that even these, among which were Professor Clapp's *Economic Aspects of the War* (see above) and Dr. William Bayard Hale's[33] *American Rights and British Pretensions on the Seas* (New York: McBride, 1915), were admittedly sober and remarkably detached studies, exceeding the general run of British-financed works in "objectivity" by many magnitudes.

In the citing of Bernhard Dernburg (his name was spelled "Dornburg" in the press release reprinted by the *Times*) the Army's censors had finally centered upon an authentic German propagandist, a citizen of Germany and a former member of the Imperial German Government, and one of the two men in the U.S.A. in charge of the entire German propaganda operations — but only through May, 1915. Dernburg was a former Colonial Secretary who had come to Washington in an official capacity along with Geheimrat Heinrich Albert of the Ministry of the Interior, as part of the staff of the German Ambassador to the U.S.A., Count Bernstorff, arriving here late in

August, 1914.

Dernburg and Albert constituted virtually all of their makeshift propaganda ministry here, outnumbered by a legion of British and their American support team. Their tiny output, though amplified by assistance from allies in the U.S.A. such as Viereck, was simply swamped by weekly Niagaras of production in this department in behalf of the British and their "allies," ultimately joined by the U.S.A. some 2-1/2 years later. Millis, in his *Road to War,* Squires, in his *British Propaganda,* H.C. Peterson, in his *Propaganda for War, 1914-1917* (Norman, Okla.: University of Oklahoma Press, 1939), Lasswell, in his *Propaganda Technique in the World War* (New York: Knopf, 1927),[34] Grattan, in Chapter II of his *Why We Fought,* and Sargent, in his *Getting US Into War,* have described variously the almost comically-one-sided contest between British and German efforts at mobilizing American sentiments between August, 1914 and April, 1917.

Dernburg authored a succession of pamphlets, and newspaper and magazine articles, in the nine months of his presence in the U.S.A., which appeared in a variety of sources, some with wide circulation. Others were published by the Germanistic Society of Chicago, and by Viereck's Fatherland Corporation in New York City. Especially bothersome to his adversaries was the one entitled *Search-Lights on the War,* which dwelled embarrassingly on the British share of responsibility for the precipitation of hostilities in August, 1914.

One of his actions got little attention for some time after it took place. Dernburg made the decision[35] which led to the publishing in New York newspapers in the spring of 1915 of warnings to Americans not to take passage on British ships sailing into war zones around the British Isles; one was published the day the *Lusitania* sailed, May 1. When this liner was sunk six days later by a German submarine off the coast of Ireland, it precipitated the first big crisis between the American and German governments, as the loss of 128 Americans, about two-thirds of all American civilian loss of life on foreign vessels in the entire war, occurred with its sinking.[36] This also led to the end of Dernburg's tenure in America, as he returned to Germany the next month.

In 1917 an ambitious French propagandist specializing in international law in Paris drew up a list of 762 persons designated as enemies of France, whom he declared to be "war criminals," one of whom was Bernhard Dernburg, and whose trial subsequently, it was hoped, would result in a sentence of forced labor for life. It was just one of a series of such incandescent manifestoes which came to absolutely nothing at the conclusion of hostilities (see Read, *Atrocity Propaganda,* Chapter X). But Dernburg's prominence on this proscription list undoubtedly testified far more to his effectiveness in the field of published works in Germany than to any connection being made at the time to his part in the *Lusitania* affair, still largely an uninvestigated matter, and having virtually no bearing on Franco-German relations.

And it was in this capacity as a writer that he once more came to the attention of Americans, and enjoyed the distinction of making Secretary Baker's third list of authors unacceptable in U.S. armed forces libraries, after having taken no part in American affairs for well over three years. After a long absence from publication in the U.S.A., a review-article of his which had appeared in a Berlin newspaper had been considered important enough by the editors of the American magazine *Living Age* to have it translated and printed in their issue for July 27, 1918. It consisted of a sustained commentary accompanying his review of a small book written about President Wilson by Professor M.J. Bonn; Dernburg's essay was entitled "What Does Wilson Want?" This was the only current publication of his in circulation, but likely to be read by a highly educated minority, as *Living Age* specialized in featuring English language translations of the press of the non-English-speaking world.

In the case of Edward Lyell Fox, the censors had on their hands another journalist with extensive residence in the areas which would ultimately become America's enemy in the spring of 1917, considerably more than Doty, Bennett and others. Born in 1887, he had joined the staff of the New York *Sun* in 1908, and remained there through 1911. He was supposed to have become vice president and managing editor of something called *Wildman Magazine and News Service* on January 1, 1912 (a periodical unlisted in the massive, approximately 6,000-page *Union List of Serials*). But he first came to public attention as co-author (with "Doctor" Armgaard Karl Graves) of a sensational book issued late in 1914 by McBride, Nast & Company, *The Secrets of the German War Office* (see the discussion of this book in note 18 above).

A few weeks earlier, while still in his 26th year, Fox had become an accredited war correspondent, with the outbreak of the war in August, 1914, for the respected *Forum* and *Illustrated Sunday* magazines, though his dispatches appeared in newspapers as well. He was known to have made at least three trips to Germany prior to American entry into the war, but it was not known how long he had stayed there after each visit; it would appear that his residence there was quite substantial.

The first fruit of his tenure at the war fronts in book form, under his own name, at least, was *Behind the Scenes in Warring Germany* (333 pp.), issued in 1915 by McBride, Nast & Company (also the publishers of "Doctor" Graves and I.T.T. Lincoln). Mystery started to gather about Fox as he flitted about wartime Germany and its frontiers. He was one of the very few Western reporters who covered at least part of the warfare on the Eastern Front involving Germany and Imperial Russia. Vague allegations that he had composed atrocity propaganda for the Germans began to be heard in 1915 and 1916,[37] supposedly things which had happened on the Eastern Front, but nothing substantial was ever demonstrated of this kind.

In 1917 two more works of his were published in the U.S.A., *The New Gethsemane,* a 66-page booklet originally published in the journal *Women's World,* and *Wilhelm Hohenzollern and Company,* also a McBride, Nast release (237 pp.). This latter book was also issued in London in 1918. By the time this happened, Fox had returned to the U.S.A. once more and the country was in the war. A year before he became one of Secretary Baker's targeted writers of "German propaganda" unfit for American Soldiers to read, Fox, ironically, enjoyed the rank of Captain in the U.S. Field Artillery.

And bringing up the rear was the only book during all this stir and excitement which had been withdrawn from sale by the *publisher* at the request of the Army, a reference book entitled *Two Thousand Questions and Answers about the War,* a 372-page cooperative publication effort by the very reputable firm, Review of Reviews; it was already in a second edition when it complied with this pressure.[38]

Seemingly it was one of the most useful general books around, and resembled in part a volume entitled *Stead's War Facts* (also arranged in a question and answer format), issued by the publisher Henry Stead in Melbourne, Australia at the very end of 1917. Just what "facts" the Secretary of the Army's Office found to be "German propaganda" in this Review of Reviews compendium got no publicity. Said the Boston *Transcript* of *Two Thousand Questions* in an editorial review on July 31, 1918, "no single volume with which we are acquainted gives so much information about the war as does this book."

It is perhaps worth one more look at the barred literature from still another vantage-point, while contemplating the Army Department's's strictures against it all as "German propaganda": that of the contemporary professional book reviewers. Roughly a third of these designated works were so scarce that they were difficult to find in most libraries. Another third though somewhat more accessible were largely ignored when published, almost entirely neglected by book reviewers and somewhat localized or regionalized in distribution. The remaining third were issued by major firms, widely marketed and read by many, and in most cases drawing multiple reviews and extended commentary nationwide, in the largest papers and magazines. These books, almost entirely produced in the years of American neutrality—1914, 1915 and 1916—are what ended up segregated as "German propaganda." A hasty glance at what the reviewers thought of most of these books at the time they first became available is in order.

The contemporaries did not call them "German propaganda," or recommend their avoidance in lieu of some 100% pro-British-or-French tract, which rarely if ever were designated in the slightest as "propaganda." Though most reviewers brought it up if the German case or interpretation of events was expressed in a favorable way, after this was noted we find no exhortation that they be destroyed or placed in quarantine, or even disbelieved. Even Theodore Roosevelt in the early months of the war placed his stamp of approval on everything coming out regardless of the side involved. Writing in the magazine *The Outlook* for September 23, 1914 the former President declared, "as regards the actions of most of the combatants in the hideous world-wide war now raging, it is possible sincerely to take and defend either of the opposite views concerning their actions." (Quoted by Grattan, *Why We Fought,* p. 37.)

Von Mach's *What Germany Wants* (1914) was considered a "temperate" answer to this question by reviewers; the New York *Times* described this book by a Harvard graduate and American citizen as "a calm, good-tempered attempt to place the German position in a favorable aspect before American eyes." And his much larger follow-up, *Germany's Point of View* (1915—see note 20) was held by reviewers to be "a restrained defense of Germany," while again the *Times* found that it had "the merit of being written with rare self-control and reasonableness of spirit."

Professor Burgess, late of Columbia's political science department and writer on many subjects, took much abuse later, but his *European War of 1914* (1915) was cited without hostility as having a pro-German interpretation of the *origins* of the war and of being only mildly anti-British, while expressing the conviction that historically Germany had been a "better friend" to the U.S.A. than Britain. Later on it was thought inexplicable by some that an American academic with no German blood or German ax to grind should have adopted such positions, but they surely had substantial merit, and postwar revisionists on the origins of the war came far closer to Burgess' contemporary views on the subject than they did to those of "Allied" partisans.

Frank Harris' *England or Germany?* (1914-1915) *was* scored by reviewers for being decidedly pro-German, but this was ascribed to his Irish ancestry. Nevertheless they were impressed that he came down on the German side objectively as a social system, maintaining that the Germans had done more in the previous twenty years for Western civilization on the whole than any other people had ever done before in that much time; this was a distinctive approach to the conflict in the view of critics.

Hedin's *With the German Armies in the West* (U.S. ed., 1915) was criticized by what were obviously pro-British reviewers in the U.S.A., disregarding that the book was originally intended for *Swedish* readers, and tried to tarnish its general import by suggesting that his was an account guided by the German high command, which let him see only what they wanted him to see, but undoubtedly his unqualified denial of ever witnessing any atrocities or harsh treatment of prisoners of war or civilians was the thing mostly resented: this flatly contradicted what was being widely disseminated by "Allied" atrocity story peddlers in this high-water atrocity story year of 1915.

Henderson's very brief *Germany's Fighting Machine* (1914), though praised as "compact," "useful," as well as by several other commendatory adjectives, was also designated as a pro-German interpretation of the war's origins, but what seemed to be most objectionable was his scathing estimate of the British diplomatic alliance with Imperial Russia as "the most monumental act of folly in modern history." (In all this immense conflict over the merits of various books on the war and its participants, there was nothing published dealing one way or another with the fortunes or ambitions of Imperial Russia; somehow the "Allies" failed to impress Americans with this important partner, concealed its part in bringing on the war, and helped to sustain ignorance in America on it all, which contributed to making the upheaval in the Eastern sector such a surprise when it finally occurred in 1917.)

Granger's realistic appraisal of the British Empire (1916) apparently stimulated *ex post facto* estimates of its influence mainly resting on his stiff objections to an alliance between Britain and the U.S.A., and as such was considered a principal counter to the widely publicized and praised proposal by Professor Roland Greene Usher, *Challenge of the Future: A Study in American Foreign Policy* (Boston: Houghton, 1916), which vigorously advocated such an alliance, and an American abandonment of "isolation." But again Granger's emphasis was on American interests, not hostility to those of others.

Reviewers of Howe's *Why War?* (1916) did not stress the pacifism others found in the work later. What they picked out at the time of publication was his analysis of the world economic forces causing the war, his criticism of British world domination and his kind words for the German seeking of a "place in the sun," sufficient to cause a reappraisal 2-1/2 years later as a work of "German propaganda." Again, as when dealing with von Mach and others, the 1918 censors utterly ignored in Howe's case his earlier *Socialized Germany* (New York: Scribner, 1915), which contained warmer sympathies for Germany than the work which made their list. Reviews of the latter title noted that Howe's sentiments approximated those of Harris of the same year, in which the former concluded that "no other country has so greatly improved the well-being of so large a portion of the people" as had Imperial Germany in the generation prior to the European war of 1914. How the searchers for works with kind views of Germany managed to miss this one additionally complicates the problem of understanding.

In the case of Hugins' *Germany Misjudged* (1916) the reviewers saw on the author's part efforts to dispel among Americans such visions, encouraged by Germanophobes, of the Germans as being monsters out to "conquer the world," and with the determination to flaunt such tyrannical ambitions in perpetuity. But they tended to find his analysis of the war and the world close to that seen in the writings of such English critics as H.N. Brailsford, George Bernard Shaw and especially G. (for Goldsworthy) Lowes Dickinson. (When the latter published an extension of already publicized views the following year, *Choice Before Us* [New York: Dodd], the American reviewers registered vociferous approval, while the British views of their countryman were sour and critical.) However, American reviewers of Hugins thought he had done a superior job at outlining his view of a better postwar world in another book, *Possible Peace: A Forecast of World Politics After the Great War* (New York: Century, 1916). The New York *Call* described the latter book as "pacifist," even though Hugins recommended a postwar U.S. standing army of 400,000 and a navy second only to Britain's. Of Hugins' *Germany Misjudged* the *New Republic* said in review, in 1916, "this kind of verdict lies nearer to the judgment that history will pass on the war." (Hugins' concern over the endless accusations from British propagandists that the Germans were trying to "conquer the world" suggested that such allegations were all from one side. But there were others who simply turned this around, the one seeming to draw the most blood being that by Professor Ferdinand Tönnies, *Warlike England As Seen By Herself* [New York: Dillingham, 1915]. The New York *Times* in its review of Tönnies on January 2, 1916 summed up the author's thesis, which it thought excessive, to be: "England has always been guilty of an overweening lust for world conquest.")

Reviewers had a field day scoffing at Lincoln's *Revelations* (1916), which contained a spread of claimed experiences and adventures across a span of European geography so large that the whole labor was bound to stimulate dubiety. One reviewer was impressed by Lincoln's assertions as to the degree of culpability of the British Foreign Secretary Sir Edward Grey for the outbreak of hostilities in 1914, a matter dwelled on at length the year previous by Morel and Neilson. (The opposite view of Grey from the British war establishment viewpoint which seemed to be most heavily stressed while the war was in progress was James W. Headlam's *History of Twelve Days,* issued in the U.S.A. by Scribner in 1915, a justification of the maneuvering of Grey in the decisive time between July 24 and August 4, 1914.)

Two books by Irish partisans drew wide reviewer interest. That by Margaret Skinnider, *Doing My Bit For Ireland* (1917) was dealt with as a narrative utterly devoid of involvement in the European war, by a school teacher and suffragette, wounded in the rebellion of April, 1916 and an ultimate migrant to the U.S.A., a spirited account which made a "German propaganda" list by the strangest of processes. In the case of McGuire however there were extenuating circumstances growing out of his geopolitical views. In his *What Could Germany Do For Ireland?* (1916) attention was called to his views sympathetic to Germany on the grounds of his conviction that a triumphant Britain would never grant Ireland its independence while a victorious Germany might; one reviewer thought that McGuire believed Ireland would be a major beneficiary of a German victory. But this sentiment had been detected even more broadly by reviewers of his previous book, *King, the Kaiser and Irish Freedom* (1915), another book escaping the 1918 censorship team, which reverberated with pro-German support, all linked to Irish ambitions. However, one reviewer noted that McGuire tempered his views by reiterating his looking forward to the U.S.A. being an "arbiter" helping settle conflicting claims at the end of the war, and that this possible role was being endangered by "Allied" protagonists who were "distorting" the nature of the war and making a possible participation of the U.S.A. along lines he looked forward to precarious. McGuire's two books were marginal in the matter of being "German propaganda," but purely by default; without Britain's obtuse and chaotic handling of the Irish scene there would have been little if any basis or reason for the pro-Germanism in McGuire's books.

As for estimates devoted to books by authentic German nationals, it was reviewers who called attention to the author of *The Emden* (1917) and other books in English translation about the adventures of this German warship and crew in 1914 as being the ship's first officer, a man who impressed even American Navy men, but no one assayed *Kapitänleutnant* von Muecke as a German propagandist. When it came to Professor Muensterberg however there were wild variations among the reviews of *The War and America* (1914), ranging from evaluations of the book as "replete with errors" to being a "well reasoned and plausible" account. Like several non-German writers Muensterberg found his homeland not to blame for the outbreak of the war and the Russians and French primarily culpable in much the manner of the postwar diplomatic history revisionist investigators. And like some other Americans he thought the U.S.A. would stay neutral and would one day by the arbiter and mediator of the war.

On the books by American journalists and others who spent considerable time in Germany in the years 1914-1917, a couple of whom were there far longer than Hedin, the complaint by some reviewers was about the same. They simply saw no atrocities or mistreatment of prisoners of war in Germany. This was especially so of Mary Ethel Macauley's *Germany in Wartime,* which finally saw the light of day here in 1917. Here it separated into American versus British reviewers. In the U.S.A. they were almost all kindly, while the ones printed in London were very hostile, especially that in the *Times Literary Supplement* of April 4, 1918; that in the New York *Times,* by the late date of March 17, 1918 with the U.S.A. being at war with Germany almost a year, sounded slightly like those abroad. At issue was the same subject and complaint registered against Hedin and Doty: Macauley reported no atrocity stories, and her accent on positive issues made her sound as though she were trying to make a case for Germany's internal situation. The British reaction provides another inkling as to how she ended up on Secretary Baker's list, even if she did not have anything to say about Ireland. As to Fox's book

Wilhelm Hohenzollern & Company (1917), one of the products of the author's visits and stays in Germany, which largely was devoted to sketches of the Kaiser, the Crown Prince, and such political and military figures as Bethmann-Hollweg, Hindenburg and Ludendorff, it was well regarded by reviewers here. Typical was that in the New York *Call* of August 19, 1917 which admired the book and thought it the work of a cool, calm, impartial investigator, even if it was past the time for such people, with the war fever climbing noticeably in the land.

As for the authors and books Grattan believed were under suspicion by the Wilson regime's other investigators, not counting the two which made both lists and have already been examined, the two which drew most reviewer attention were those by Labberton and Naumann. In the case of the former's *Belgium and Germany* (U.S. ed., 1916) it gave testimony to the persistent exploitation of the German invasion of Belgium as well as the atrocity tales which grew from the short military campaigns in that same month of August, 1914; it was difficult to separate these themes. Labberton, holder of two doctorates, and a professor at the University of Groningen, came under attack primarily for maintaining that the invasion of Belgium by the Germans was not "illegal" in the sense of violating any lawful treaty consideration; it was his view that the 1839 treaty cited to the point of total exhaustion by pro-war British partisans (Morel made a hash of this during the war and Grattan some dozen years after hostilities an even bigger one) was no longer binding in 1914. Critics such as Labberton stressed that the treaty had been renewed for one year in 1870 at the time of the Franco-Prussian War and nothing had ever been said about it in the nearly 45 years after that. Furthermore the original treaty did not commit signatories to go to war with other signatories who chose later on to consider it no longer in effect or binding (it can be assumed that Professor Labberton as a Dutchman was acutely conscious of the part played by Britain and France in carving this new buffer state of Belgium out of southern Holland in 1830).[39]

The remaining title, Naumann's *Central Europe* (1915) drew by far the most reviewer attention in that year. Though there was then and later some trouble in spelling the names of the author and the German title of the book correctly here and there, in a dozen major reviews even the British were not hostile. The main theme of this work was concerned with the possibility of a union or federation of states stretching from Turkey and the Balkans to include those of northern Europe, with the Germanic peoples as the nucleus, but with the sovereignties of all respected, effecting a political and economic understanding and joint cooperative enterprise. One American reviewer praised it as "the most famous book to which the war has given birth."[40] And in other attention to works issued in 1915, reviewers of the collection of essays on Germany written by Professor Schevill made the point that the entire work had been put together several months before the war had even begun.

By far the majority of the writers who were convinced the German interpretation of the *origins* of the hostilities was correct, or more correct than the British-French version, were content to carry the matter to that point. Their views on the possible outcome were much mixed and tended to lean toward one vision or another of a hoped-for negotiated peace short of any total victory by anyone, with the expectation that a still-neutral U.S.A. (at least through early 1917) would exert a significant influence on a peace settlement acceptable to all belligerents. Even a profound Irish protagonist such as McGuire, as we have seen, who tied his hopes for Irish political independence in the future to a German military victory, was ambivalent here, as he also favored this above desirable outcome, based on an American presence leading to a non-military settlement, which obviously was an alternative to a predominance of German arms.

Something in the nature of magic or a miracle had taken place if we note the situation which existed anywhere from two to almost four years later. Without these authors or publishers having done another thing to their work during the passage of all this time, what had been looked upon when happening in 1914, 1915, 1916, and early 1917 as contributions to the enlightenment and education of the American citizenry on the subject of the war in Europe and the related world politics had been converted wondrously *ex post facto* to propaganda in behalf of the enemy at the late date of September, 1918. Though this did not quite compare with the celebrated Comte de Saint-Germain (see the 11th edition *Encyclopædia Britannica,* vol. 24, p. 5) and his alleged achievements in transmuting lead or the like into gold, the event did represent a remarkable conversion of something into something else, probably even more impressive in that it was all so intangible and psychological. The ability to detect this remarkable transformation surely indicated the possession of the most incredible talents, powers and sensitivity on the part of those announcing these intellectual discoveries, but why it took such a long time to tell the country about it all no one ever got around to explaining.

The administrative history of this nearly-forgotten expedition into the thickets of literary suppression is another subject. The story of how Army post and public libraries coped with the official edicts and private pressures growing out of this affair would take a vast labor to reconstruct. The purpose here has been the identification of the authors, titles, publishers and something of the content of the items tagged for sequestration or destruction, within the context of the events of the time, and related at least to a minimum of the total situation. There are several spin-offs of this entire event worthy of additional attention, ranging from reactions of publishers to the scapegoating of their publications, to responses by authors upon finding themselves spotlighted in national attention on charges of having produced propaganda for a wartime adversary. Nothing of this appears to have been done at the time. Like so much else that was quickly directed into oblivion with the sudden end of hostilities on November 11, 1918, this happening vanished as though enveloped in ten tons of concrete and dropped in the Philippine Deep. But those made more curious by the consequences of intellectual curiosity may find it worth pursuing further as additional possible consequences and ramifications come into view upon additional rumination and investigation.

Afterword

When Secretary of War Newton D. Baker issued his directives of late summer and early fall of 1918 ordering the removal of 47 published works from U.S. Army post and camp libraries as unfit for the soldiery to read, he opened up an immense subject, potentially. This was especially true after his action spilled over into the civilian sector, and public libraries about the land, without official direction, began to weed out, impound and/or destroy these same 47 publications. The Army's action was obviously not intended to have this result, but, as it worked out, it had perhaps an unexpected public-sector compliance with serious implications for general civil rights and civil liberties, even if public awareness of this at the time was almost imperceptible. What Secretary Baker really achieved was to open up the vast topic of what the citizenry of the United States might read about many aspects of the war—during the war. It is amazing that there was no real measurable contemporary reaction to this, no extended speculation as to its possibilities and general implications. It is equally alarming that the whole matter was settled simply by neglect, undoubtedly assisted by the general feeling of relief and euphoria set loose by the ending of the war just a few weeks after the entire incident was initiated and precipitated.

One of the more obvious implications of the Army's move against the stipulated 47 published works was that what remained in libraries or elsewhere after these had been removed were perfectly satisfactory for the armed forces to read, and that the book stacks had been officially cleansed. An active enemy propaganda ministry, had there been one, would have exulted in high glee over this entire affair, as the censorship decision overlooked a formidable library of works with a far greater potential for infecting the readership with unwanted views and convictions than what had been formally suppressed. In this number of the submerged and the low-profile were at least three dozen books with known or suspected sponsorship by the German government through American representation itself, let alone an immense swath of publications by Americans with no known German sympathies at all who simply expressed views and convictions mainly or entirely out of sympathy with the war, the way it was being conducted, and those who were conducting it. The political and ideological variations in all this literary product were astounding, and bewildering; the variations emanating from the pacifists and the "Peace" movement alone almost defied analysis and categorization.[41] One stands in amazement and amusement at the pretensions of these essentially political-amateur dabblers in censorship, upon contemplating what a mere scratch on the surface of the problem they were really etching. However, what should have disturbed and unsettled contemporaries was the potential for what was *not* done, and what *might* have been done, had there been in charge an element which really knew and understood what they were *doing*.

The failure of this incident to arouse interest from chroniclers of the war may be due in part to the relatively undramatic nature of the episode when ranged against the far more absorbing and distracting contemporary tales of combat, and, later, the complicated postwar world politics which captured popular attention. Secretary Baker and the entire cast of this intellectual interlude are missing from the substantial book by H.C. Peterson and Gilbert Fite, *Opponents of War, 1917-1918,* though there is excellent coverage of other aspects of censorship during the 19 months of American war involvement. The entire incident is also missing from the famed compendium *Banned Books* by Anne Lyon Haight (New York: R.R. Bowker, 1955). Though this is here and there interested in books banned in wars, in the main it is concerned with censorship for other reasons and at other times. Some later compilers of bibliographies of suppressed books are also completely ignorant of this affair. The whole business quickly slipped away and interest in the momentarily notorious books lists evaporated to the point where one might imagine they ended up in an Orwellian "memory hole" designed just for them. It would be a very tiny club indeed were one to gather together whatever industrious souls as could be found who had recollections of these authors and their forbidden works.

Despite the feebleness of memories and the abysmally short fashion of historical memorialization, there is a recurring psychologico-political phenomenon involved which should attract attention. Wars follow wars, and there are broad general courses of action which reappear even if they never quite follow in precise details. Differences may induce those who experience them and the intellectual impositions they incur to think that nothing previous to their time matched what they went through, which may be one of the reasons that during the "light-switch" statecraft of the adversarial-confrontational state system the same impositions or even worse variations thereof can be made generation after generation as the war seasons come and go. What gets banned or suppressed may change profoundly in content but the procedures remain the same. There is a tendency for them to become more sophisticated with aspects of covert psychic intimidation of varying degrees of subtlety carried out in such a way that there is little awareness that censorship and suppression of intellectual freedom is taking place at all. There are analogous things taking place in war propaganda itself, changing from a bald-faced telling of lies to a telling of just part of the truth, or a simple total suppression of news or facts without any perceptible indication of this one way or another.

We might for instance examine a few of the on-going tendencies in book suppression in the quarter of a century or more after the events we have concerned ourselves with above. Mrs. Haight did devote parts of two pages of her treatise on book-burning-and-banning to the famed ceremonial conflagration in National Socialist Germany, initiated on May 10, 1933 (*Banned Books,* pp. 121-122), while the purely political gesture involved was underplayed. One of history's outrageously over-exaggerated events, looked at from the perspective of 55 years, surely has been this incident in 1933, immensely exploitable because it was so explicit (see note 42, below). But compared to the conflagrations involving literature across the centuries including the era previous to printed books, which have involved countless libraries in many lands burned to the ground (a fire in the U.S.S.R. National Academy of Sciences in Leningrad on February 14, 1988 destroyed or badly damaged 4,000,000 books), this event in Germany would barely rate a footnote. The exigencies of world politics since then have resulted in the assigning of a value to this incident as though it were the only event of its kind. Like other footnotes in history which have been tortured and bent out of shape to replace the main text it persists in the repetitious conditioning so peculiar to the photographic 20th century, gawked at over the decades of television-watching, and less understood every year it is recalled. Against the total backdrop of literary suppression for all reasons across the ages it is a mere curiosity. However, as do all suppressions, for whatever reason, this one has given some of its targets an intellectual life far beyond what several of them had any right ever to expect.[42]

But Mrs. Haight went on to demonstrate indirectly that this event in terms of total achievement in the destruction of politically undesirable books was an inconsequential bagatelle when compared to the achievements a decade later of the Anglo-American adversaries of Germany in yet another war, when "Allied" saturation bombing of the famed German "book city" of Leipzig destroyed a vast number of books, far more than any zealous supporter of Adolf Hitler had ever dreamed of torching in May, 1933. Mrs. Haight also proceeded to discuss actions of the Coordinating Council of the American Military Government in postwar Germany in directing wholesale removal and pulping of books, from stores and libraries, which reflected favorably upon the defeated National Socialist regime, or even upon the older traditional German nationalism, for that matter. However, her prize commentary was reserved for the Communist regime of East Germany two decades after the 1933 bookburning incident, in 1953, when Communist cultural watchdogs removed from book stores, schools and libraries *five million* books, an action which reduced the Nazi ceremony of May 10, 1933 to the level of a mere prank by comparison (*Banned Books,* p. 123).

Americans were not total strangers to the practice of suppression and large-scale destruction of books, but for reasons quite apart from the political. The career of Anthony Comstock (1844-1915) had ended just a short time before the U.S. Army action was precipitated in 1918; he was the most zealous and indefatigable pursuer of "immoral" or pornographic literature the land has ever known. As a special agent for the U.S. Post Office between 1874 and 1915, Comstock had been known to confiscate such printed works at the rate of over 30 tons in one year or another, probably much of it borderline or questionable when it came to being explicitly offensive according to the standards maintained by the postal services in harmony with public law of the time, particularly in the quarter of a century after Reconstruction.

But this was part of a long, ongoing program, and though execrated by recent generations of liberal critics it did have extended and broad public support in the time it was sustained as public policy. This campaign resulted in constant trials of authors, publishers, distributors and dealers of literature considered morally reprehensible. Comstock claimed to have prosecuted and secured the conviction of almost 4,000 persons in four decades, though publicity also sharply increased sales and demand for titles which drew public attention during all these proceedings in court.

These legal actions also had a long period of influential impact afterward, especially in the operations of various urban organizations enforcing "decency" by pursuing "vice" incorporated in books, best known through such as Boston's Watch and Ward Society and the New York Society for the Suppression of Vice. At the time of the furor over the political action against Communist and other books in Germany in 1933 there was simultaneously an intense campaign being waged against "obscene" books in New York City and State, by the Legion of Decency. It was the New York City Public Library which had removed George Bernard Shaw's *Man and Superman* from its shelves in 1905, and it was in the same city where the most vigorous efforts were being made to prevent the publication of James Joyce's *Ulysses* in 1933.

In the U.S.A. the relatively coarse and inexact pursuit of political and ideological sin imbedded in books which has been observed in the narrative of the transactions in the closing months of World War One was not repeated in the war of 1939-1945, about 30% of which was also sat out of as a non-belligerent. But there occurred a silent attack on literature this time which started almost with the European war declarations of September 1939 and which program still needs its chronicler. Just between December, 1940 and December, 1941, the last calendar year of American "neutrality," U.S. postal authorities seized *over 600 tons* of foreign publications at West Coast ports alone, which were "destroyed at these ports of entry," according to the bible of the publishing industry, *Publishers Weekly* (September 5, 1942, p. 832). The story went on to complain that, in addition, "Many libraries, particularly university libraries, had consignments of books from abroad seized and destroyed from September, 1939 down to Pearl Harbor" [December 7, 1941]. This separate annihilation of books obviously dwarfed anything attributed to the German enemy this second time around in less than a generation.

In addition to the remarkable diligence and energy of the Post Office Department in destroying books from abroad at U.S. ports of entry, there was another form of interference, again hitting the university and research facilities: the quarantining indefinitely of periodicals, with nothing said as to when they might possibly be received by addressees. Porter Sargent, in No. 35 of his famous *Bulletin* newsletter (February 9, 1940), revealed: "Scientific periodicals now, as during the last war, are cut off from us. The Smithsonian Institution, Washington, which customarily acts as a clearing house for foreign exchanges, has forwarded no periodicals since August, 1939. The War Documentation Service, Philadelphia, R.H. Heindel, Director, tells us that a Joint Committee on Foreign Relations, N.Y. Public Library, has arranged for foreign agents to hold in storage scientific and scholarly periodicals that cannot be forwarded because of the embargo." And the country was still almost two years away from involvement in the war as a formal belligerent. From belligerency onward, the interception and destruction of vast quantities of printed works from abroad at all ports of entry can only be imagined in terms of scope and volume, let alone value.

Domestically, however, the program ran quite in the opposite direction, operationally. During 1941-1945, American books were not amassed and destroyed *after* publication. They were "burned" in manuscript, *i.e.,* they were simply suppressed by prospective publishers while in typescript or holograph form, and did not get loose to illuminate the citizenry and bedevil and upset or anger the wartime establishment (several books critical of America's Stalinist "ally" did not make the light of day until well after the end of this war). This of course was a policy of self-censorship on the part of the publishers; there was no official policy requiring this.

A major statement in how this was to work was made as early as March, 1942 by Bennett Cerf, president of two major publishers, Random House and Modern Library, and head of the largest book-distribution organization in the United States, the Book of the Month Club. Part of his effort was in laying down the ground rules for the coming brainwash of the country with respect to Stalinism and the Soviet Union, now that the fortuitous course of hostilities had thrown the U.S.S.R. and the U.S.A. into their queasy comradeship of an unstable military alliance of sorts. On the general book business in war and the agency of self-censorship in behalf of political and military compliance, Cerf had this to say:[43]

Book publishers, in signal contrast to some of our most powerful newspaper proprietors, have been meticulous so far in keeping from their lists any new titles that might contain sly or poisonous propaganda. Scripts are read with rigid care. In some cases, books already printed and bound have been junked at the last minute, and the resultant losses written off without a murmur. Booksellers, too, should maintain a constant vigil over new publications. If any one publisher inadvertently or by design, slips through a single book that preaches a creed inimical to the war effort, the retailer will be performing a service to his country by deliberately sabotaging that book.

And following up that ferocious totalitarian credo, Cerf delivered himself of this closing testimonial which helped readers of *Publishers Weekly* to understand the ideological origins of his entire position in support of his bid to become our prime literary commissar:[44]

The publishers and the bookseller should check backlists carefully. The fortunes of war have brought into being alliances that looked incredible only a short time ago, and have proven that some of our most cherished theories were utterly false. Our old conceptions of the Russian purges and trials, for instance, and the Russo-Finnish war, evidently, were mistaken, and books that encourage those beliefs should be taken off sale immediately. Russia is a friend in need to us today. People who dangle the menace of Russian Communism constantly before us are increasing our chances of losing the war. Let us deal with our so-called menace of American Communism after the war is over. I say, "so-called," because, in my opinion, American Communists are a singularly ineffective and insignificant minority.

With people such as Cerf in control of the book publishing business, one need not wonder that the U.S.A. in World War Two needed no censorship apparatus nor a corps of printed-word bloodhounds to sniff out and destroy anything within book covers which might incense or affront the sensibilities of those directing the "war effort," whether Stalinophiles or not.

Six months later the editors of *Publishers Weekly* felt that the message needed to be re-asserted in general terms, while pointing out that just negative repression had been abandoned as a control device in favor of a positive employment of the publishing business to sell the wartime Government's program rather than as a damper upon the expression of independent ideas on that or any other view which might come up in this land of irrepressible individualism:[45]

During the course of the war much of the book censorship which will be brought to bear will be silent and inarticulate .... The book trade will wisely try as much self policing as possible, and make official action unnecessary. The democratic censorship of responsibility can be made to work in the Second World War as it did in the first .... Publishers will keep a sharp eye on books which might run afoul of the censor, but their main emphasis will be on books as morale-building agencies. This dynamic and positive aspect of the role of publishers in wartime is instanced in the creation of non-governmental organizations, of which the Council on Books in Wartime is an important example.

The First World War in the U.S.A. was an era of the wildest proliferation of intellectual freedom imaginable compared to World War Two. Nothing within a light year of the Government's program in the First was ever dreamed of in the Second, as the expert techniques in the formation of lock-step perfected in the 25-year interim precluded any possible independence of mind to get loose for more than a few moments, let alone flourish even to the degree in which it did in 1917-1918. The relatively chaotic unconformity of the former time never came within a peep of repeating in the latter. The mass compliance which prevailed, had it taken place in an era or a land with a social system based on chattel slavery, would have been looked upon by its main political beneficiaries as the answer to a slave-holder's dream. Americans will be a very long time getting over the psychic drag created and built in by World War Two, let alone hope ever to live in a political world which has escaped its shadow.

If one chooses to retreat deeper into the past instead of working forward while examining the phenomenon of book destruction, perhaps a different perspective will be gained, and a somewhat more genial estimation of one's own time may result. Since we are dealing with a brief incident in a topic which would result in a library-sized stream of volumes if the entire subject were examined by the required multitude of investigative scholars, the total picture since the perfection of any kind of writing probably could not be even *read* in a lifetime, let alone written in the lifetimes of the many hundreds who might be required to have done the writing. What can we make for instance of the campaign of the Manchu emperor Kao Tsung, who undertook to expunge totally from the literature of China all works containing critical or derogatory references to the Manchus and their "northern predecessors"? Between 1774 and 1782 he is credited with the direction of a book-hunt which resulted in the extirpation of over 2,000 *titles* from the book collections of the country; the total number of individual volumes involved cannot even be wildly guessed at (*An Encyclopedia of World History* [Boston: Houghton, Mifflin, 1948], p. 541).[46] Hoping to learn of every such event since anyone ever recorded anything for posterity is undoubtedly just one of many possible intellectual exercises which would dizzy even the most imaginative. Stopping grievously short of such an achievement, in full understanding of what might possibly be the "full" story, is a practical way of concluding such an investigation as this.

Notes

1 Baker was the second Secretary of War in Wilson's Cabinet, replacing Lindley M. Garrison, who had resigned early in February, 1916.

It is obvious from Secretary Baker's middle name that he had some German blood. It has been commented upon at various times that the part played by Americans of partial or full German descent in bringing about the defeat of their ancestral country twice in global wars in the 20th century, primarily for the benefit of third, fourth and fifth parties, was not only vast and unprecedented, but unmatched by any other people, and the performance in the war of 1939-1945 was far more lethal and destructive than in that of 1914-1918. Though the U.S.A.'s largest continental European ethnic strain, German-Americans participated in it all with the casualness of a housewife pouring hot water on an ant-hill, and the involvement of very many men with German forebears in the American armed forces in positions of high rank has been a subject of wide notice over the years. Taken in the context of a racial and/or ethnic rather than a national or patriotic fact, it is worth a modicum of pondering. It will be granted that most of the people involved were one to three generations removed from Germany physically and culturally as well as psychically, but in the cases of people of British or French ancestry in America, for example, separation from their motherlands even by one or two centuries has had little effect upon the intensity of their affections for their ethnic origination point. In the light of all this, for sure, the brass of others to refer to those of German origins as "hyphenates," while casually ignoring the much stronger tug of inheritance upon the other peoples making up the American population, has been a remarkable demonstration or reflection of dissembling partiality and warped prepossession.

2 New York *Times,* September 1, 1918, Section 2, p. 2. The headlines read:

MANY BOOKS BARRED FROM ARMY READING

SECRETARY BAKER ORDERS DESTRUCTION
OF LONG LIST OF TITLES IN ALL LIBRARIES

SOME BY FAMED WRITERS

PRO-GERMAN BOOKS KEPT IN PUBLIC LIBRARY
FOR STUDENTS, BUT NOT FOR CIRCULATION

3 The contemporary historian of the War Library Service was Theodore W. Koch. See his *War Libraries and Allied Studies* (New York: Stechert, 1918) and *Books in the War: The Romance of Library War Service* (Boston: Houghton Mifflin, 1919). For what the WLS suggested and promoted as proper reading in service libraries see also Koch's *Books in Camp, Trench and Hospital,* shorter edition (Ann Arbor, Mich.: University of Michigan, 1917); extended edition (London: J.M. Dent & Sons, 1917).

4 New York *Times,* January 17, 1918, p. 22.

5 New York *Times,* March 29, 1918, p. 4.

6 The cooperation of the civilian sector with the Army Department censors in their prohibitions of various books and pamphlets in the late summer and early autumn of 1918 is not a fundamental aspect of this study, and is only incidentally noted. The full story of how the public and possibly private librarians and libraries in the U.S. weeded out their book stacks, in harmony with pressures brought upon them by local chapters of the American Defense Society, would undoubtedly make quite a voluminous if not a multi-volume report. The reaction in this writer's adopted home city of Colorado Springs, Colorado is considered sufficient for the purpose at hand, though it has been seen that in New York City there was an immediate transfer of the Army book banning to the local civilian library situation, and an instantaneous investigation of the possibility of the forbidden books being available to non-Army readers.

In Colorado Springs, a mainly mountain summer resort small city of less than 30,000 population in 1918 (on this city one should consult the remarkable book by Marshall Sprague, *Newport in the Rockies*), the local chapter of the American Defense Society got to work quite late on the Army's book list. It was almost two months before it was revealed that the ADS branch would take up the matter of the books in question with the city's Library Board. According to the afternoon newspaper the list of the books either was requested or sent without request from the office of the Secretary of War but was not received until the end of October. The *Evening Telegraph* of October 29, 1918 (p. 5) announced, "PLAN PURGING OF C.S. LIBRARY SHELVES OF PROPAGANDA BOOKS"; "Local Defense Society Receives List of Volumes Barred By Secretary Baker Because of Hun Tone."

The list originally published September 1 was reproduced exactly as it had been promulgated, errors and all, but there was no mention of the supplementary list of September 25. Though nothing was said about action by the Library Board, apparently there was an almost panicky desire to cooperate, for but three days later the Librarian, a Miss Lucy Baker, reported that such books as were on the list that were in the public library had been "removed." As the *Evening Telegraph* of November 1 (p. 16) reported, with satisfaction, "NO HUN BOOKS OR PROPAGANDA IN PUBLIC LIBRARY."

This cleansing of possible intellectual contamination fit in well with an action of three months earlier. A few days before the beginning of the 1918-1919 school year the teaching of the German language was expunged from the entire school system, presumably at the request of the student population itself. As the *Evening Telegraph* of August 7, 1918 (p. 10) disclosed, "German textbooks and everything that savors of Fritz will be barred from the Colorado Springs High School and all the public schools during the coming year. The students have refused to have anything further to do with the Germans or anything that pertains to them. The few who have studied the language last year were busy apologizing for it most of the time. R.C. Hill, Superintendent of Schools, stated this morning that he was glad the students refused to have the study of German included in their regular High School course." In actuality, maybe as many as 200 American communities had already discontinued the teaching of German by the time action on these lines took place in Colorado Springs. On the course of this trend down to March, 1918, see H.C. Peterson and Gilbert Fite, *Opponents of War, 1917-1918* (University of Wisconsin Press, 1957).

The total uprooting of the German language in America as an accompaniment to the quasi-total-war approach of the Wilson war government had ramifications which were as obdurate and obsessive as were the complete-eradication objectives of those who intended to eliminate German culture eventually in the world. One of these variations had paying for the war partially in mind, that of the famed Bostonian literary light, Ellery Sedgwick, editor for thirty years (1908-1938) of the esteemed magazine, the *Atlantic Monthly.* In the summer of 1917, Sedgwick, instead of recommending like others the extirpation of German, urged that a tax be placed on every word of the German language which appeared in print in this country. With the German language press already in grave retreat, and soon to be almost wiped out, the linguistic exterminationists seemed to have won the field. No tangible hostility to Sedgwick's suggestion was registered, with the exception of a blistering private letter to Sedgwick from Albert Jay Nock, then a some-time published magazine journalist, and whose literary career was almost entirely ahead of him. Nock's letter of July 14, 1917 to Sedgwick is reproduced in Francis Jay Nock, ed., *Selected Letters of Albert Jay Nock* (Caldwell, Idaho: Caxton Printers, 1962), pp. 88-91, and is summarized by Robert M. Crunden, *The Mind and Art of Albert Jay Nock* (Chicago: Regnery, 1964), pp. 138-139.

[7] Peterson's and Fite's *Opponents of War, 1917-1918* gives January 17, 1917 as the publication date of *The Finished Mystery,* placing it in advance of the American declaration of war by some ten weeks, but there is extended internal evidence to the contrary in materials published by the group which released it. Judge Rutherford authorized the compilation which resulted in the book, and he did not replace Pastor Russell as president of the organization until January 6, 1917 at which time the authority to do this was acquired.

[8] Rutherford and his seven colleagues were charged with violating the Espionage Act, and were eventually convicted of this, but the original charge by the United States Marshal at the time of arraignment sounded like a violation of the Selective Service Act: "the offense of unlawfully, feloniously and willfully causing insubordination, disloyalty and refusal of duty in the military and naval forces of the United States of America when the United States was at war," in addition to distributing "a certain book called Volume VII, Bible Studies, 'The Finished Mystery,'," and other

publications. This is quoted from the Transcript of Record of the trial in *Jehovah's Witnesses in the Divine Purpose*, p. 79, note *n*. This work contains much of the material in this account pertaining to the history of the suppressed book, most of it compiled from contemporary organizational publications, and reissued by the Watchtower Bible and Tract Society in New York in 1959. *The Finished Mystery* was the seventh in a series by their Pastor Russell, and though posthumously published seemed to have been planned as far back as 1906.

9 See New York *Times,* June 22, 1918, p. 18 for the account of the sentencing of the eight men. The *Times* ran an editorial in approval of this action on p. 6 of this same date.

10 Time had already come down on the side of the Russellites. With the failure of the U.S.A. to be a party to the Versailles Treaty and with Senate repudiation of joining the League of Nations, action ending the state of war was unilateral. Though one may date the shooting war between the U.S.A. and Germany from the war declaration by the former on April 6, 1917 to the establishment of the Armistice of November 11, 1918 the state of war between the two countries went on long after that. These 19 months were followed by 36 more during which a technical state of war persisted. As Professor Edwin M. Borchard, Hotchkiss Professor of Law at Yale University, pointed out, in his book with William Potter Lage, *Neutrality for the United States* (New Haven: Yale University Press, 1937), pp. 278-279, formal peace really did not begin until the ratification by Congress of the Treaty of Berlin on November 11, 1921. (There were some very interesting economic activities of the United States Alien Property Custodian during the three years of post-shooting-events, partially described by the above authors. The continued state of technical warfare provided the legal excuse for the above-mentioned official to continue for a long time the confiscation of property owned by German citizens in the U.S.A. In one instance, that consisting of thousands of patents, it led to the accruing to Americans for a long time after the war of advantages and benefits resulting from access to all this which would not have been possible had Congress simply terminated the war as easily as they had launched it in the first place, as Borchard and Lage suggested, by a simple resolution at the end of 1918 repealing the declaration of war. The fate of American property in Germany during this same time has drawn no attention of significance.)

11 In designating the books on the War Department's banned list as German "propaganda" the Secretary of War was using the word in its martial-political context. Even the works on the list which might have been described as favoring German objectives avoided the *atrocity* aspect of propaganda, a very special form which superficially appeared to be wholly subjective but had many other and quite long range objectives. On the surface there may seem to be disadvantages to complaining about being victimized by the enemy's violation of accepted behavior in wartime, mainly serious negative consequences for morale. It may appear to be a superior course to ignore such acts even if they *do* occur, substituting for the exploitation of such the adoption of an attitude of strength, reflected in such declarations as "No one and nothing can hurt *us!*"

On the other hand the continuous recitation of atrocities one is alleged to have sustained may have a hard-headed and long-view goal behind this apparent effort to recruit sentimental sympathy from others. Carried along systematically it is obviously very useful in building a bank account of psychic and emotional support, in attendance upon some time in the future when it can be spent in achieving a variety of very tangible material considerations and concessions from a presumably defeated adversary, apart from purely vengeful aims such as achieving the murder of an enemy's leadership class. Once a commonplace consequence of defeat, in the much more hypocritical modern era subtle excuses for achieving this design have replaced this tactic, with prior behavior becoming an excellent pretext for dispatching the more stubborn and implacable of the conquered opponents.

12 New York *Times,* September 26, 1918, p. 24. The news story simply reported that Secretary Baker has ruled that the 16 books were "unfit for American soldiers to read."

13 The writings which ended on the Army ban exploiting biblical analysis and prediction concerning the meaning of the war which started in 1914 were but a fraction of the total, and attention to this in this context is necessarily abbreviated. An early example, appearing in 1915, was the 115-page essay by one D.W. Langelett, *World War in the Light of Prophecy,* published by the German Literary Board of Burlington, Iowa, which did not sound like a religious operation. "In-the-light-of-prophecy" analyses, discourses and interpretations abounded during the war.

14 New York *Times,* May 14, 1916, Sec. I, p. 1 *et seq.*

15 The world should long remember the Brothers Maxim. Maine-born Hiram (1840-1916) was the inventor and perfector of the first true "practical" machine gun in 1884, introduced widespread in most of the world's armies well before the First World War broke out (see the astounding article on the machine gun by Major Charles Francis Atkinson, later famed for his English language translation of Oswald Spengler's *The Decline of the West,* in the 11th edition of the *Encyclopædia Britannica*). Hiram's younger brother Hudson (1853-1927) was the holder of a large number of patents on various explosives, some of which were employed with impressive results in the high explosive shells of World War I artillery. Deaths and wounds in that war caused by machine guns and HE outnumbered by far all other responsible agents except for fatalities and disabilities caused by disease.

Though nitroglycerine had been invented before he was born, and though he was just a boy of 10 when Alfred Nobel detonated dynamite, Hudson Maxim by the approach of American entry into the war in 1917 had become a formidable figure in the high explosives business, had taken a prominent part in the "preparedness" agitation, and had created a major corporation to produce and distribute his lethal products. Hudson Maxim had been the first in this country to make smokeless powder, in 1888, a process adopted by the U.S. government in 1901 and which he subsequently sold to the du Pont combine, for whom he eventually went to work. Among the younger Maxim's innovations was "Maximite," the first high explosive to penetrate heavy armor plate. His scare book *Defenseless America,* a 318-page work brought out by Hearst's International Library in 1915 (his brother Hiram's autobiography *My Life* was published by McBride the same year), had a major impact but, like its author, seemed to make little impression on historians. (The Maxims have virtually disappeared from the record.) A subsequent chore Hudson Maxim performed for the arms and ammunition business was a brief worked up for the American Defense Society, *Colossal Folly of the Proposition for the Government to Make All War Munitions,* which the ADS distributed out of their Fifth Avenue address in New York in 1917. For a sense of the relationship between patriotism and profit, few were in the league of the American Defense Society.

It would be entirely appropriate to acclaim Hudson Maxim as the Founding Father of "defense." Though the sums spent on weaponry and the wondrous machines and apparatus today far exceed even the most expansive dreams of 70 years ago, and have been a deeply-rooted part of the social system for 50 years, much of what one reads and hears on a daily basis sounds as though paraphrased if not lifted directly from *Defenseless America.* Though armament and potential adversaries have changed, the "defense" language of the modern confrontational-adversarial system testifies to the almost timelessness of the analysis and visions of Hudson Maxim.

16 It is a tribute, however, to the deep and lasting psychic influence of "Allied" propaganda to note that even Millis, writing 17 years after the end of the shooting war during the high-water time of post-1918 revisionism, still could not shake himself free from the deeply implanted prejudice that there was something reprehensible, almost, about anyone writing in an adversarial manner to British war politics, and that there was something "tainted" about the work of such writers during the period of American neutrality as Frank Harris, William Bayard Hale and Professors Clapp and Burgess. Though Millis frankly admitted the objective quality of much of what these men wrote, nevertheless he still expressed indirectly in his *Road to War* the opinion that they were border-line reprobates while the admitted "thousands" of others grinding out ridiculously-slanted materials for the British war government were presumably of a morally superior cast. That such pre-disposition was universal in the U.S.A. helps to make understandable how the country by and large swung so swiftly, so smoothly and so profoundly to the British side once President Wilson, who won re-election in 1916 on a stay-out-of-the-war platform, almost effortlessly engineered American entry into the war four months later.

17 In view of the pacifist works which did end up on the Army list it strikes one as strange that for the most part the substantial production of American pacifist writing was ignored, including the largest part of the big names. One cannot see any trace of such as Norman Thomas and associates in the National Civil Liberties Bureau, the pacifist pamphlets written by William Jennings Bryan and Clarence Darrow, or such works as R.M. McCann's *War Horror.* Nor was there any sensitivity to marginal works of mixed socialist-pacifist tendencies and impulses one finds in writers of much fame in Britain who were widely read here, such as H.N. Brailsford's *War of*

Steel and Gold, first published by Macmillan in 1915 and which had gone through *nine* editions by 1917, including those by Bell in England, or H.G. Wells's *The War That Will End War* (Wells's *What Is Coming?,* issued in the U.S.A. two years later by Macmillan, predicted a deadlock in the European war, and peace resulting from mutual exhaustion), or the output of the socialist publishing house of Kerr in Chicago, such as the economist Achille Loria's *Economic Causes of War,* translated from the Italian by John Leslie Garner and issued in the U.S.A. in 1918. Probably the most fatefully-titled work by the anti-war people in this time was Wells's *The War That Will End War,* published in New York by Duffield in 1914. Transformed during the ensuing combat by propagandists into the slogan "make this the war to end war," it became a target for many grim and sardonic comments in the succeeding two decades.

18 There is little doubt that of all the over-inflated reputations of any and all participants in war, those of spies and espionage are the worst. Especially to the point is Phillip Knightley, *The Second Oldest Profession: Spies and Spying in the Twentieth Century* (New York: Norton, 1987).

In his discussion of World War One spies and espionage, Knightley does not concern himself with Lincoln, but devotes a page to a contemporary with some strange and mysterious similarities. This was "Doctor" Armgaard Karl Graves (a pseudonym), whose sensational book *The Secrets of the German War Office* was published by the firm of McBride, Nast & Company in New York late in 1914. The following year it was reprinted twice, again by McBride, Nast and in London by T.W. Laurie, Ltd.

Its literary quality was almost entirely the result of the work of a 26-year-old journalist, Edward Lyell Fox. After about four years with the New York *Sun,* Fox was apparently largely engaged in freelance writing when he was contacted and employed to spruce up and make readable the memoirs of "Doctor" Graves, a feat he achieved in a few weeks, getting it to its publishers a short time before the war broke out in Europe in August, 1914. (Knightley identifies the main author only as "Dr. Graves," does not mention his first and middle names in his index nor the title of his book in his bibliography, but does give Fox credit for the work in making it literarily presentable.)

The book was undoubtedly fast-paced and engagingly readable after Fox's efforts, and got widely praised for these qualities, but the exotic and unlikely nature of many of its anecdotes and narratives puzzled and in some cases soured other reviewers. One simply could not believe the Kaiser would spend so much money in such devious capers as "Doctor" Graves described to locate information commonly available to anyone able to use a library; the reviewer for *The Independent* considered it a collage of lies about everyone, while the New York *Times*'s reviewer maintained that it could have been written by almost anyone with moderate writing skill and possessing a smattering of knowledge of public affairs and European history from 1900 or so onward, as well as an imagination sharpened by assiduous reading of Sherlock Holmes and "Nick" Carter detective stories. Graves's book actually enjoyed a run as a series of magazine articles in 1914 published in *Collier's Weekly,* which led to a question raised by the second New York *Times* reviewer, an anonymous history professor who had many objections (December 13, 1914, Sec. VII, p. 565). Among other things he deplored the numerous misspellings of German proper names and places, which led to doubt whether the repeated mistakes were those of Fox, and whether they preceded or followed magazine serialization. The second critical review in the *Times* concluded with a reproduction of a letter from the German Ambassador in Washington of November 19, 1914, dismissing Graves's book as "pure fiction." Knightley's assessment nearly 75 years later was in harmony with the 1914 contemporaries who thought it quite worthless and unbelievable.

Knightley declared it sold 50,000 copies but it did far better than that. The London edition of 1915 announced it was in its 90,000-copy printing, a new edition lacking Fox's name on the title page was simultaneously available in America, and the book continued to be available for at least another dozen years; it was still in print in the U.S.A. in 1928. Strangely enough it was translated into the Cyrillic alphabet and issued in Czarist Russia in 1915 as well, and still another edition was published under Soviet auspices in Moscow, apparently an abridgement of the 1915 edition, late in 1944, during still another war with the Germans. A second book attributed to "Doctor" Graves, seeking to capitalize on the subject and the war, *The Secrets of the Hohenzollerns,* also issued by McBride, Nast in New York and London in 1915, did not fare anywhere nearly as well.

Lincoln's *Revelations of an International Spy* came out so closely on the heels of "Doctor" Graves (who apparently is still unidentified), and issued by the same publisher, that it did arouse a few comparisons and suspicions. Not only did both authors spread a large number of improbable yarns about spying, and have the same publisher. They both had been convicted of offenses and served time in British prisons prior to the issue of their books in Britain, and the British government had disdained in both cases to prosecute them as spies, even though both had been mainly involved in claimed pre-war espionage in behalf of Imperial Germany.

19 Lincoln's incredible career accelerated rather than subsided with time. Deported from England after serving his shortened prison sentence on August 11, 1919, he surfaced in Holland where he visited the German Kaiser living there in exile, and issued a plea for the restoration of the monarchy in Germany (New York *Times,* August 12, 1919, p. 15). He next came to the attention of the general public as official censor of the postwar provisional government of Germany, and left the post precipitately, to surface in the postwar states of Czecho-Slovakia, Austria and Hungary, where he ran into trouble in all of them. Once more in the United States, the German authorities accused him of participation in the 1920 Kapp Putsch in their country, but by the mid-'20s there were no further pending charges. On the heels of all this he next emerged in China during the incredible events in that country's 1926-1927 emergencies, and, following that, in 1931, it was rumored that he had become a Buddhist monk. (It might have been recalled that when Lincoln was arrested in New York in 1915 on a British complaint, he had claimed then to having posed as a Buddhist monk in Central Asia before the war of 1914 on some vague espionage assignment, and that he threatened to return there in the same capacity to foment trouble for the British, "to get even with England." So there may have been conjecture as to whether this latest news represented a real "conversion" to Buddhism or a belated return to an old subterfuge in a gesture in fulfillment of his 1915 threat.)

20 An example of the obtuseness of the censors surfaced at once when examination revealed that von Mach had produced a book almost three times the length of *What Germany Wants* the very next year (1915), issued by the major Chicago publisher McClurg under the title *Germany's Point of View*. Why the much briefer treatise published in 1914 should be featured on the Army's prohibited list and the far more comprehensive work of the following year on the identical subject should have been totally disregarded is just one of a lengthy list of imponderables growing out of this entire incident.

And von Mach went on to contribute what amounted to a third effort of this kind by providing a translation of the German, Paul Rohrbach's, *German World Policies,* also published in 1915, by Macmillan. The omission of this latter piece of authentic "German propaganda" from the Army list of mainly political exotica three years later was simply additional evidence to its critics of the incompetence of someone.

Since the Army's campaign was directed solely at "German propaganda" (no other ideology or intellectual heresy was ever mentioned), one might have wondered what it took to qualify for entry into this special fold. And in view of the operational strategy being entirely *ex post facto,* then there should have been far more diligence expended in making sure that the most extreme examples were appended to the list. For instance, there was the most profound and eloquent manifesto of German aims and ambitions probably ever seen here, the emotional statement by the celebrated German Professor Rudolf Eucken, "Our Righteous Cause," originally appearing in the *Illustrierte Zeitung* in Germany and published in English language translation covering a full page in the New York *Times* on September 27, 1914 (Sec. IV, p. 2). Anyone interested in protecting America's soldiery from contamination resulting from views supportive of the adversary in 1918 should surely have put this issue of the *Times* on the Secretary of War's list, but nothing of the kind took place. A contemporary might have been excused for standing back in consternation at the neglect of the possible influence of someone with the eminence of Professor Eucken (1846-1926), decorated with international distinctions, which included the 1908 Nobel Prize for Literature.

On page 164 of Phyllis Keller, *States of Belonging: German-American Intellectuals and the First World War* (Cambridge: Harvard University Press, 1979), there is a brief reference to a law suit against the publisher Macmillan by von Mach, settled out of court in 1921, over the failure of the publisher to bring out his diplomatic documentary anthology. The circumstances surrounding this are confused, but it would appear it *was* brought out, and what happened to it during the war became the issue. Following is the entry in *The United States Catalog Supplement—Books Published 1912-1917* (New York: H.W. Wilson Co., 1918), p. 1236:

> Edmund Robert Otto von Mach (1870-), ed. *Official Diplomatic Documents Relating to the Outbreak of the European War: With Photographic Reproductions of Official Editions of the Documents (Blue, White, Yellow, etc. Books) Published by the Governments of Austria, Hungary, Belgium, France, Germany, Great Britain, Russia and Serbia*; introd., daily sum-

maries, cross references and Footnotes.
0 xxii, 608 [707] p. $6. S '16 Macmillan

[21]Actually only about 20 pages of the total of 60 in *Songs of Armageddon* were devoted to verse extolling the German cause and related sentiments, or "allegiance to Germany and the German cause," as noted by reviewers of this work in 1916 and early 1917. In terms of total wordage, this was the briefest work to make Secretary Baker's banned literature list two years later.

In one of Viereck's anonymous articles published in the *Saturday Evening Post* for June 22, 1929 a virtual library of works was mentioned, none of which ever graced the Army list of "German propaganda." Among them were mentioned works which could not be located, including a book tentatively entitled "The Case Against Armed Merchantmen," "The War Plotters of Wall Street," an untitled work attacking munitions shipments to the Allies by Viereck, several pamphlets by Bernhard Dernburg (see below) and a satirical deflation entitled "Trip Through Headline Land," which appeared in 1915 and concerned the repeated and false announcements in American newspapers of the continuous "annihilation" of the German army, a work purportedly by "the author of the Catechism of Balaam, Jr.," which probably was, again, Viereck himself. Some of the Dernburg material was issued by the Germanistic Society of Chicago and distributed by Viereck through his Fatherland Corporation located at 202 East 42nd Street in New York. Also distributed by Viereck was *The German White Book*, the English translation issued by the Imperial German Government in August, 1914 and published by Oxford in New York in 1915.

[22] The interlock among von Mach, Schrader, Muensterberg and Viereck is dealt with in part by Keller (see previous note) and also by Elmer Gertz in his *Odyssey of a Barbarian: The Biography of George Sylvester Viereck* (Buffalo, N.Y.: Prometheus Books, 1978). The contributions to *The Fatherland* are especially interesting, and involved the expression of sentiments by the authors which were somewhat sharper and more pro-German than in the works in book form which were ultimately selected for special attention by the Army, with the possible exception of some of the verse in Viereck's *Armageddon,* which was forthright in its pro-German sentiments.

It was strange that though Germans were early world leaders in clinical psychology and had Americans traipsing to Germany to participate in the earliest that they should have been so ineffective in perfecting the arts of propaganda. It was the eminent William James, according to Porter Sargent in his book *What Makes Lives,* who brought Professor Muensterberg from Germany to establish the U.S.A.'s first psychology laboratory.

[23] Those who were profiting from the vast industrial buildup, first for "preparedness," and then for the war itself, abominated respectability to anything he wrote (Millis in *Road to War* [p. 303] remarked that "nobody who mattered" read Nearing's pamphlets). But over 20 years later, when Senator Henry F. Ashurst of Arizona in a Senate speech in August, 1940 reminded his rapidly dwindling listeners in the Senate that World War One had created 23,000 new millionaires in the U.S.A., all this despite the effect of an income tax which had gone into effect the year before

the war began, maybe those few folk about the land who remembered those stormy days of 1917-1918 might have finally realized what Professor Nearing was talking about in that dim past time. Senator Ashurst's figure was an adjustment upward from that released contemporary with the events just transpired. According to figures made public on April 18, 1920 by the Treasury Department (cited by John Kenneth Turner, in his 1922 book, *Shall It Be Again?* [New York: Huebsch], p. 284), "the war created 21,000 new American millionaires," while revealing in addition that "during the war period, 69,000 men made more than three billion dollars over and above their normal income." There was never any attention given to possible fortunes made out of World War One by non-citizens and residents abroad. In addition, since this attention was focused on *new* millionaires there were no statistics released which concentrated on what the war bonanza did to enhance upward the fortunes of those who were already millionaires prior to the war, or what two years of "preparedness" before formal belligerence might have additionally contributed to all this spectacular new opulence.

[Historians writing about money in the past are frequently struck with a sense of futility in trying to impress those of a later time as to the importance of a given sum or the attainment of a particular income level at some previous occasion, or the impact of population growth and inflation rendering the same levels of achievement later less important. In that respect the significance of the past has been defeated, since there is no way to translate the experiences and situation of the earlier occasion so that they can be understood later on. There is no better example of this than to try to make someone appreciate what it meant to be a "millionaire" in, for instance, 1918, and what this designation described 70 years later. However, this problem repeats itself over and over, in all previous or succeeding times. In June, 1988, for example, figures from the U.S. Census Bureau and Internal Revenue Service indicate that there was a millionaire in the U.S.A. for every 100 households; in other words, more than 1,000,000 millionaires for the entire country. For one inclined simply to equate this status from one time to another and assume they mean the same thing regardless of decade or era, the possibility of comprehending the past is gravely impeded, if accurate perception can be said to be even attainable in such a situation.

Perhaps a handbook incorporating the economic facts prevailing at any given moment in the past might be necessary to demonstrate to someone of a later date as to what it meant in the earlier context to be, let us say, a "millionaire," and why one who was one exerted such influence upon the events that transpired in the earlier day. (The 16th Amendment to the U.S. Constitution authorizing the imposition of federal income taxes was ratified in February, 1913. According to the Commissioner of Internal Revenue in 1914, only 44 persons in the U.S.A. reported a net income of $1,000,000 or more in 1913, and of the approximately 358,000 persons who filed returns, almost 84% reported a net taxable income of less than $10,000. New York *Times,* December 12, 1914, p. 9. Over a year and a half into World War One, a seven-room apartment in the fashionable Morningside Park district in New York City rented for $85 a month; a pound of fresh-ground gourmet coffee cost 20 cents. New York *Times,* February 20, 1916, p. 8.) It might be that some new tactic has to be employed to register relative significance in trying to compare things of this sort across substantial spans of time. But as long as it is possible and convenient, if not encouraged, to read history backwards through the use of the same words when they really are not saying the same things at all, there will be a fundamental flaw in the understanding at a later time in trying to grasp what took place and why, and distinctions as to why this or that phenomenon had the impact and importance that it did in a previous time will be virtually impossible to make.

When one speaks of a "millionaire" in a previous time, when wages and prices were 10 to 20 times or 30 to 40 times less than they may be when you are reading about it, you have to be aware you are not talking about the same thing when concerned with a contemporary "millionaire"; the latter is economically and politically only a shadow of the former in terms of impact and influence in decision-making, politically. When, as a matter of illustration, one considers a millionaire in the U.S.A. in 1938 as against one in 1988, in the former case you are involved with a time when there were barely half as many people, when the minimum wage was *thirty cents* an hour, and the average income of working people totalled $800 or less a *year*. A closer idea of his economic position compared to that of an apparent counterpart 50 years later can probably be approximated by multiplying his "millionaire" status by a factor of 25 or 30 or more, with even greater allowances made for an earlier time because of much lower taxes. It may very well be that expecting to get across the significance of proportionality is hopeless, though maybe another try may sound like a reasonable suggestion. And hopefully it may be appreciated that being a "millionaire" in a time when a nine-course dinner cost 65 cents suggests an impressive difference in the economic and political status of such a person, and his consonant impact on the times, when matched against a "millionaire" of a later date, when such a dinner cost $90 or more, before the obfuscators start quibbling over the respective menus.]

24 The investigation of scandals related to non-performance in World War One military procurement contracts began while the war was still in progress. Probably the most sensational was that dealing with the non-production of military aircraft.

As early as September, 1917 the U.S. public was being regaled by newspaper stories claiming that American aviators were already engaging the fliers of Imperial Germany in the skies of northern France, flying airplanes of American manufacture, which itself was being hailed as a stupendous achievement. This was an obvious untruth. U.S. Army combat fliers were there but in a trickle, and not the advance guard of a supposed 150,000 who were believed to be soon flooding the war zones. Furthermore, they were flying European-made aircraft hardly any better than what men learned to fly in, let alone engage an armed enemy in combat with.

Reports that all was not well in the plane-fabrication business kept circulating during the fall and early winter of 1917-1918, leading eventually to an investigation authorized by President Wilson. His special investigator was the famed sculptor Gutzon Borglum, an amateur flying enthusiast but a person with wide knowledge of the aeronautics business of the day, and aware of changes and improvements from personal involvement. (John Gutzon de la Mothe Borglum [1871-1941] was already famous for his statuary which was to be found as public monuments or on display in various public buildings around the country. By far his most famous work came after

World War I, the gigantic Mount Rushmore Memorial carvings of four American Presidents in the Black Hills of western South Dakota [1931].)

Borglum began supplying detailed reports to the President beginning in January, 1918 and on March 18 electrified the country with one that no American-built warplanes had yet reached the fighting fronts in France. Borglum maintained that as of that date the American plane industry, which had received immense contracts, was capable of producing 50,000 airplanes a year and should have sent to France 5,000 as a minimum at that moment, yet had failed to send overseas a single aircraft.

Apparently Borglum's drastic assessment embarrassed Wilson somewhat, and his work was abruptly concluded. Wilson then repudiated Borglum, and the latter's main report, based on nine separate investigations, was suppressed.

This angered Borglum, who subsequently staged a private press conference of sorts on Sunday, April 28, 1918, at which he not only placed on record the details of his investigations into the non-performance of the aircraft industry but recommended criminal prosecution of the Chief Signal Officer, Brigadier General George O. Squier, through whose office the contracts apparently were let. Borglum added to him a list of others, including not only the membership of the presidentially-appointed Aircraft Production Board, but a select ring of aircraft manufacturers as well, *in toto* having received close to a billion dollars in contracts without producing and delivering to that moment a single serviceable fighting aircraft. (The coverup and the excuses began almost at once, and no one seemed to be responsible for anything.)

President Wilson, apparently shaken by Borglum's ill-tempered reaction to official neglect and burial, and disclosure to the New York City press on the state of indolence and dereliction in the military aircraft industry, persisted in smothering the report and its possible impact by a policy of silence.

However, the President reorganized the Aircraft Production Board the following month, placing it under the direction of a major figure in the copper industry, John D. Ryan. And in June, 1918 President Wilson authorized another investigation of the industry. This one was supervised by the eminent Charles Evans Hughes, Wilson's opponent in the 1916 election, Secretary of State under two subsequent American Presidents, and eventually appointed Chief Justice of the U.S. Supreme Court (1930). Apparently Wilson had learned his lesson, however, and he had his Attorney General, Thomas W. Gregory, monitor carefully the work of the investigation of Judge Hughes.

The Hughes investigation was conducted between June and the end of October, 1918 and his report was made public about two weeks before the war ended. Though less critical than was that by Borglum, and while exonerating the Aircraft Production Board's civilians of any "wrongdoing," nevertheless his report came to a similar conclusion to that of Borglum, also recommending criminal prosecution of some Army officers for various acts committed in relation to their APB duties. Hughes differed from Borglum only in that the men he recommended be indicted and prosecuted were not the same as those cited by Borglum, which suggested that the circle of malfeasance was somewhat wider than previously believed. When one considers the purchasing power of a billion or more dollars 70 years ago in those small-price and small-tax days (probably 12 to 17 times what that will buy today, depending on what one might want to buy), one has an inkling as to the scope of this incredible operation.

The blare of publicity attending this sensational scandal was muted to a whisper in days, as much more dramatic news pushed it into the background: the cessation of hostilities and the end of the shooting war in Europe a week and a half later. The whole affair quickly drifted into obscurity, and, like its companion, the shipbuilders' scandal, limped into silence, dragging well into the years of the succeeding presidential administration, billions of dollars in write-offs and a mainly inconclusive termination.

(On the Borglum revelations see the front page stories in the New York *Times* for March 18 and April 28, 1918. The Hughes report was more restrained as far as publicity was concerned. It was summarized in this study from the front page account in the New York *Times* for November 1, 1918 and from news stories datelined from Washington, D.C. as reproduced in the Colorado Springs *Evening Telegraph* for October 30, 1918, p. 7 and Colorado Springs *Gazette,* November 1, 1918, pp. 1,3.)

25 Nearing was a pamphleteer in the Second World War as well as the First. In downtown Boston in 1944 this writer encountered a person on a street corner handing out copies of his *Who Are the Peace-Loving Nations?* Apparently annoyed and repelled by Secretary of State Cordell Hull's wearying repetition of the expression "peace-loving nations" in a speech earlier preceding the start of the Dumbarton Oaks sessions at which were laid the groundwork for the creation of the United Nations, Nearing had arrived statistically with the evidence, and with some wit and irony demonstrated, that the "peace-loving" Anglo-Russo-American "allies" had been involved in several times as many wars as the German, Italian and Japanese enemy of the moment.

26 Scott Nearing's place in American intellectual and social history remains an obscure question mark, as his views have for some time become unfashionable. Though an exponent of collectivistic solutions for many problems for over two generations, he remained a solitary and fiercely individualistic, unorganizable personality, to the regret perhaps of "reform" organizations of many kinds, as had been ruefully recounted by Professor Louis Filler, writing of Nearing in his *A Dictionary of American Social Reform* (New York: American Philosophical Library, 1963), pp. 533-534. Speaking of Nearing's impressive stream of published writings, Professor Filler concluded, "His remarkable productivity was not matched by increasing influence; his sharp independence, coupled with his persistent radicalism, and perhaps increasing bitterness toward a country which had withheld honors from him, apparently separated him from mainstreams of liberalism or radicalism." Philosophical and ideological differences aside, it is indeed a display of a mean-spirited and ungenerous trait of a social system to act as though a man who continued to make intellectual contributions well into his ninth decade in the world did not exist or had not existed.

27 The symposium *Conquest of War* attributed to a writer named M.M. Thomas and others could not be located. The *United States Catalog* indicated no such titled work issued in the U.S.A. during the war years, nor was a copy in the Library of Congress. (There was the possibility the Army list had transcribed the name wrong and that the writer was Norman Mattoon Thomas [1884-1968], one of the headliner writers in the pacifist camp [see note 17] but no wartime bibliographies listed a work by him with this title. In the succeeding half-century Thomas went on to become one of the best-known figures in American public life.) This was also the experience in trying to locate the anonymously published *Free Speech and a Free Press*. There were many works incorporating variations of this title, such as the well-known pamphlet *Freedom of Speech and of the Press* by the redoubtable Reverend John Haynes Holmes, published in 1918 by the National Civil Liberties Bureau in New York. (There was an article of this identical title by W.R. Vance also published at about this same time, in the March, 1918 issue of the *Minnesota Law Review.*) What the pre-war travel and adventure writer Lawrence Mott could have produced in the field of propaganda also could not be determined.

28 Cronau, 62 years old when the Justice Department agents confiscated his book, had been distributing it for years from his home at 340 East 198th Street in New York; it averaged two editions a year, and sold for $1.

29 When Grattan first conceived of his strategy for writing about American involvement in the First World War a decade after it was over, he thought of producing a trilogy: *Why We Fought, How We Fought,* and *What We Got.* He eventually wrote and published only the first of the three. Essentially, however, one must concede that this approach is about what one can devise as worth saying subjectively about involvement in any or all wars.

The precipitous decline of the reputations and fortunes of such first-rank revisionists as Harry Elmer Barnes, Grattan and several others from the post- World War One era of 1920-1940 or so well down after the end of World War Two was accompanied by a new assessment of the earlier war by an element which largely dismissed the bread-and-butter issues emphasized by Grattan and others and substituted such spooks as "national honor" and "national interests"; this was characteristic of the new way of thinking encouraged by the megalomania dominant between roughly the Cold and Vietnam Wars, of the period 1945-1965. A part of this new version being presented a generation utterly innocent of the previous approach was accompanied by a malice toward the earlier examination and proponents which reached what could be described as new heights or new depths, depending upon one's perspective. Grattan, in a moment of exasperation and incensed by the discourtesy he was encountering at one time while engaged in attempting to sell part of his library to a major university, exploded to Barnes in a letter of July 15, 1964: "It is being borne in on me that the American academic establishment is a crappy indoctrination racket, manned by a trivial and ignorant lot of bums with whom I could not be comfortably associated even for money."

Grattan's profound contempt for the new dispensation in "hire" education was slightly modified five years later when Bobbs-Merrill brought out a new edition of his *Why We Fought* upon the 40th anniversary of its original publication, on which occasion he found that there was at least a slight strain of newcomers to the Halls of

Poison Ivy which thought his work had sustaining merit and held up sturdily as a narrative and interpretation of the 1914-1917 pre-war years in the United States. Grattan's Afterword to the 1969 edition of his book is distinguished writing.

30 Atrocity propaganda is helpful in stirring indignation and hostility at the start of a war, inducing mass involvement emotionally, from whence derives subsequent mass armed forces enlistment. (In tiny conflicts between the professional armies of rival dukedoms of, say, the 16th century or earlier this was quite unnecessary.) Atrocity propaganda is also very helpful after hostilities have begun, fueling hate and energy for the continued prosecution of the war, and once the enemy is sufficiently de-humanized (see Lasswell, below), he simply cannot be suffered to live. (General J.F.C. Fuller argued in his *The Conduct of War, 1789-1961*, published in London by Eyre and Spottiswoode in 1962, that the objective of war was to get the enemy to stop fighting, not to kill everybody, but this can easily be turned aside and the latter enthroned as the sole objective, with enough effective atrocity propaganda.) Finally, there is the pay-off. Assuming that there is a "winner," atrocity propaganda against the loser (only a loser commits "war crimes" and the like) performs an essential task in paving the way for the programs of killing selected members of the defeated side, and the subsequent appropriations of lands, money, property and other material con-siderations which really lay behind the conflict to start with. To head off the above kind of analysis the accumulators of the vast loot involved always conduct an impla-cable attack on those who take part in such politico-socio-economic dissection, employing brigades of journalists, professors and Explainers, who seek to suffocate these critics with clouds of abstract ideological goof-gas; it rarely fails to work. Sometimes it resembles the re-cycling of the original propaganda, turning it upon the unconvinced, in their rectitude, in a modified form, after it has served its original purpose. Only in the case of wars fought to a draw or ending in negotiated peace is atrocity propaganda quite limited as a decisive accessory and auxiliary agent.

31 The circumstances attending Labberton's book approximate those attending Hedin's: intended for a neutral European readership, this time Dutch. Its English lan-guage translation by W. Ellery Leonard and issue here by Open Court of Chicago in 1916 was well in advance of American belligerence. That it had a pro-German lean in their controversy with Belgium probably spoke more of the long-standing many-sided Dutch-Belgian division, probably best seen in the French-Flemish split long exploited on religious and linguistic lines in Belgium. Its part in the war allegiances would seem to be more or less incidental. It was after all only 153 pages long. The suspected title by Muensterberg this time was a big book, written well before the war began, and, like Reventlow later on, was intended for an exclusively German audience. Translated into English by Edwin B. Holt and published by the publishing giant Doubleday in 1914, to be suspected of being German-financed was enough to make even an Anglophile wince. The question to ask might have been what Profes-sor Muensterberg had to say about Americans which would cause a major American house to think it worth reading here. Similarly amusing was the notion of Lewisohn's *Spirit of Modern German Literature* as some kind of smuggled-in Teu-tonic-financed propaganda; the book actually was a compilation of the author's lectures on the subject before an audience of University of Wisconsin students and issued by Huebsch in 1916. In the case of Naumann, the inquisitors were again suggesting a ludicrous scenario: another book long before published in Germany as *Mittel Europa,* translated from the German by Christabel M. Meredith and issued in 1917 by the major house of Knopf. Like Muensterberg, it surely was a case of having been brought into existence originally by German money, but in Germany and at a time long before it was anyone's business in the U.S.A. whatsoever. Russell, one of the youngest of these writers at the time, might have been classified as one of the more moderate British writers on the war, along with Angell, Brailsford, Ponsonby, Morel, Lowes Dickinson, and possibly Wells, but to be suspected of German financing again was an imagination-stretcher. Open Court in Chicago brought out his *Justice in War Time* in 1916. (It is true that occasional reviewers found *Justice in War Time* to be too "pro-German" for their tastes, but if the people suspecting publication auspices were alert, they would have demonstrated far more zeal in examining Russell's next book, *Why Men Fight* [New York: Century, 1917].) That same year another major Chicago publisher, McClurg, issued Ferdinand Schevill's *The Making of Modern Germany.* Professor Schevill, a distinguished professor and voluminous writer of European history at the University of Chicago for over a generation, put together this book from a series of six public lectures he had delivered in the city of Chicago the previous year of 1915. (It would appear that Professor Schevill's sole effort in behalf of a kind word for Germany took place right at the start of the war in Europe, when the Germanistic Society of Chicago published his 15-page pamphlet, *Germany and the Peace of Europe,* in 1914.) [In this writer's opinion Professor Schevill's history of the city of Florence is one of the three great books he has encountered in 60 years of serious reading of history, and Professor Schevill himself the most outstanding intellect of the first 40 years of this century he was privileged to meet personally.] Zangwill's *War for a World* was a large book of 455 pages and issued early in the war; what Macmillan published in 1917 was a revised edition. Zangwill enjoyed the strange distinction of being accused of having written propaganda for *both* sides in World War One.

32 The idea that President Wilson's intellectual investigators might suspect that German money underwrote a book by the Englishman Bertrand Russell was exotic enough. That they would also suspect such sponsorship of a book written by a Member of Parliament was indeed a flight into the outer reaches. But it was on the list of suspects as indicated by Grattan: how Francis Neilson's *How Diplomats Make War* could be under Justice Department conjecture and also escape the Army Department's list of forbidden books is a further incomprehensible lapse.

The story of how this book, one of the two in this entire essay which still has a substantial readership today, made its appearance in this country, has been told in various ways, but it was obviously not a product of the ordinary literary traffic. The work had been prepared by the author while an elected member of the House of Commons, and smuggled out of Britain in manuscript by his fellow Georgist compatriot Albert Jay Nock, ending up in the editorial offices of the New York publisher Huebsch.

Its first publication was in November, 1915, a month before Neilson resigned his House seat. Neilson's name was not on the title page of the first edition; its author was identified by the simple pseudonym, "A British Statesman." Had it been otherwise, Neilson stood a good chance of being arrested and ultimately sentenced to a substantial spell in prison. A second edition came out in May, 1916, and a third printing in January, 1918, well after American involvement in the war. It appears that it is from this time that it began to draw intensive interest, though it would seem that British Intelligence and its auxiliary arms should have begun its investigation with its first appearance two years before. Neilson's drastic indictment of the British Foreign Office for its part in bringing about the precipitation of hostilities in August, 1914 should surely have made this a prime target for suppression and destruction.

How Diplomats Make War became a standard, coming out again in 1921 and once more in October, 1940, and additionally since with no indication of a new printing date. This was well after a second world war in a generation was underway. Though Neilson was an accomplished writer in several fields, this work probably was classified by some as journalism or "amateur" history, but it drew solid praise from one of the academic world's most famous revisionists, Harry Elmer Barnes (see his *The Genesis of the World War* [New York: Knopf, 3rd ed. 1929], p. 739), as did a similar essay in revisionism by Nock, *The Myth of a Guilty Nation*, published after the war, in 1922, also by Huebsch, derived mainly from the work of another British revisionist, E.D. Morel.

It is obvious that Nock, and very likely Neilson, both learned much from Edmund D. Morel (1873-1924). A member of what was to become known as the Independent Labour Party, Morel had aggravated many with his series of scathing books denouncing the behavior of the European colonial powers in Africa, beginning well before the 1914 war. Morel was one of several who did not accept their government's version of the origins of the diplomatic breakdown leading to the shooting phase beginning in August (among whom were Lord Loreburn, G. Lowes Dickinson and Arthur Ponsonby—the latter's trenchant book, *Democracy and Diplomacy* [London: Methuen, 1915], being evidence).

Morel preceded Neilson with a fierce critique entitled *Ten Years of Secret Diplomacy* (London: National Labour Press), which saw five editions in Britain between 1915 and 1918 but which was not published in the U.S.A. until after the war, in 1920, in a sixth edition. Paralleling this was a collection of Morel's electric journalism and blunt speeches in another slugging volume, *Truth and the War*, which raised British pro-war hackles to new levels as a consequence of the three editions between July, 1916 and February, 1918, also a product of the National Labour Press.

This book also failed to be issued here during the war, but two of Morel's biting pamphlets did find American sponsorship after original British release, *Morocco and Armageddon* (Manchester: National Labour Press, 1916), and *Tsardom's Part in the War* (London: National Labour Press, 1917). Two editions of the former under different auspices appeared in Chicago in 1916, as No. 11 of Open Court's Labor and War pamphlet series, and as No. 17 of the pamphlet series of the Germanistic Society of Chicago (both appeared subsequently in German translations in Germany after the war).

94

And it was this pamphlet series that led to Morel's tenure in a British jail. Strangely enough all his works managed to escape the official censor's suppression. But where Morel got into trouble was due to his attempt to get one of these pamphlets to the famed French writer Romain Rolland in Switzerland. In so doing Morel came afoul of a technical clause in the notorious Defense of the Realm Act. He was subjected to police search and arrested at the end of August, 1917 (New York *Times,* September 1, 1917, p. 2) and subsequently tried and sentenced to six months in jail, under circumstances which were conducted without publicity. Morel was still imprisoned when the third edition of his *Truth and the War* came out in February, 1918, bearing a very kindly introduction by Member of Parliament Philip Snowden and a preface by Morel's wife, which suggested hopefully that he might soon be released from prison. *Truth and the War* did not appear in the U.S.A. until published by Huebsch in New York in 1920.

The story of the collaboration of Nock and Neilson and their founding of the celebrated journal *The Freeman,* as well as their subsequent falling-out, has been recounted at various times in the literary history of the country. There is a serious indication, however, that Nock derived the title of his famed intellectual recollections, *Memoirs of a Superfluous Man,* published in 1943, from Nietzsche by way of a page in Neilson's *Diplomats,* a product of the years 1914-1915. On page 92 of the 1915 edition, in a discussion of the intellectual turmoil sweeping Germany in the 1840s and after, Neilson had gone on to say:

> Intellectual riot was fast overcoming Hegelianism and Lutheranism; the period which must come under fundamentally false conditions when the hypocrisy and cant of society are fiercely attacked by those who are bold enough to point out where life is not lived as it is preached, had about reached its meridian. Strong men had surveyed the field before Nietzsche; Marx had done something to prepare the ground; and earlier still, Max Stirner had put in the blade of his uprooting plough; Michael Bakunin also had left traces in Germany after the disturbances of 1849. His pronouncement, "We object to all legislation, all authority, all influence, privilege, patented, official and legal, even when it has proceeded from universal suffrage; convinced that it must always turn to the profit of a dominating and exploiting minority, against the interests of the immense majority of the enslaved," found an echo in that sublime phrase of Nietzsche, *"Where the State ceaseth there beginneth the man who is not superfluous."*
> [Emphasis added.]

The State certainly had not "ceased," in 1942-1943, and therefore Nock and everybody else technically were still "superfluous." Nock in a veritable blizzard of magazine articles in the dozen years before American involvement in World War Two demonstrated his gravely jaundiced eye toward the established line on international affairs during that time, and had done anything but swallow the war-involvement line. But in *Memoirs* he revealed the persistence of his stubborn revisionist view of the First World War as well. Page 162 of the 1943 Harper edition began,

"The war of 1914 ended in an orgy of looting, as any rational being might have known it would, even if he had never heard of the secret treaties which predetermined its ending." And he went on to assert that the war then in progress would end in precisely the same manner.

33 Both Grattan and Millis had kindly appreciations of Hale, once a holder of important journalistic posts in New York, as well as a season as a foreign correspondent. The *United States Catalog* had a special note relating to Hale's role as a Wilson partisan before he became President, as well as his fundamental part in drawing together the collection of writings which was ultimately published as Wilson's *The New Freedom.*

34 By far the most expert and exhaustive student of propaganda, especially that of World War One, was Professor Lasswell, from whom everyone interested in the subject has undoubtedly learned a great deal. His master compilation of sources, with the assistance of Ralph D. Casey and Bruce L. Smith, *Propaganda and Pro - motional Activities,* published by the University of Minnesota Press in 1935, listed over 4,500 sources. In one place or another in a variety of ways, Professor Lasswell over the years stressed that the very first objective of confrontational-adversarial propaganda was the de-humanization of the adversary; after that was achieved, the schedule of objectives became easier and easier to accomplish. The attainments of the "Allies" in this department in World War One were utterly dwarfed by those reached in the subsequent war of 1939-1945, to be sure. Many of the fixations planted in the latter war were still vividly held well over 40 years after its cessation, and reinforced by endless recyclings of the various stages of that war every week on television programs nationwide, especially in the U.S.S.R. and U.S.A.

The tireless re-planting of this attitudinal poison decades after its original purpose was long ago attained, and serving no apparent new purpose whatever, has been a subject of sustained interest to students of the conditioning of the lower brackets of the popular intellect. Without a doubt the success of the campaign waged against the Japanese outranks all the others. Within a matter of months after American involvement in December, 1941 propagandists had succeeded in lowering the Japanese to the level of insects, from which point the exterminationist conduct of the war was promoted with ease, with conventional or fire-bombing of 66 Japanese cities which took hundreds of thousands of civilian lives, and culminated by the atomic bomb snuff-outs of the cities of Hiroshima and Nagasaki on August 6 and 9, 1945. The horror at all this, expressed by civilized old soldiers such as the British General J.F.C. Fuller (see pp. 390-412 especially of his *The Second World War 1939-1945,* available in various printings from June, 1948 to 1968, in the U.S.A. under the imprint of Duell, Sloane and Pearce or Meredith Press), was quickly shrugged off by the new breed of Explainers known ultimately as the "megadeath intellectuals," justified in nearly all details as necessary to "victory," in this "advance to barbarism," to use the expression of another British writer, F.J.P. Veale, in his book of this title (various printing and publishers, 1948-1969). The full bill for World War Two may not be assessed, presented and paid perhaps until into the 22nd century, barring the occurrence before then of another, even bigger, global war, which will surely have an effect on this timetable.

35 According to Gertz, *Odyssey of a Barbarian,* p. 127, the idea was Viereck's while writers before him tend to stress more the part played by Dernburg, who was the responsible figure in coming down in favor of the tactic.

36 Borchard and Lage, *Neutrality for the United States,* p. 356. Professor Borchard had been Law Librarian of Congress during World War One.

37 Among the authors on the forbidden posting of the Secretary of War only Fox, the sole journalist listed who had some experience covering Germany's Eastern Front as well, was reputed to being involved in writing or repeating atrocity stories in behalf of the Central Powers, presumably accusations against Russians which involved German soldiers. Such accounts almost never appeared in print in the U.S.A., and were intended for internal circulation in Germany. However, nothing charged by the Germans approached in sensational content what they were accused of in the West, which specialized in accusations dealing with alleged mutilations of individuals (the variations on these mutilations were numerous and wondrously imaginative).

The most sensational atrocity story of the war slipped by with barely any attention at all, and seemingly disappeared from the record in very short order; it failed to make any recitation of "war crimes" in the 1918-1921 investigations and compilations. In this case it was charged not against the Germans but against their Austrian and Bulgarian allies in the Balkans sector. And it concerned not a gruesome account of a soldier or civilian found mutilated somewhere but a charge stated as a fact that Austrian and Bulgarian forces had massacred the staggering total of 700,000 Serbian civilians, some 3,000 of them supposedly being asphyxiated by poison gas in a church in Belgrade. Virtually the only attention this account ever received from a historian was that accorded by Professor Read in his *Atrocity Propaganda, 1914-1919* (see above), and the following is all he had to say about it (p. 164):

> In the following month [March, 1916] a dispatch to the London *Daily Telegraph* via Rome announced that the Austrians and Bulgarians had committed "atrocious massacres" in Serbia — 700,000 people had perished. Killing by bayonet had been too slow, so the "villains" had resorted to the use of asphyxiating gas. In one single church in Belgrade 3,000 women, children and old men had been asphyxiated.

Professor Read gave as his source for this the Paris newspaper *Temps* for March 23, 1916. But this was not in harmony with his text. In the paragraph preceding the quoted one above, he said that other Serbian atrocity stories had originally appeared in the Swiss paper *Journal de Genève,* and then had reached London from that source, published in the *Daily Telegraph* via transmission from Rome. However, his citation omitted any mention of the specific issues of the Geneva and London papers as to details or date, and he did not state how the story had then been published in the Paris paper which was the only one he identified.

It was indeed dizzying that a story alleging the deliberate mass murder of some 700,000 civilians, some of them by poison gas, should have slipped into oblivion so quietly. (Nothing approaching a light year of this had ever appeared in the West, even in the first calendar year of the war, when the most sensational accounts were launched.) The gassing story alone should have led to a brigade of journalistic investigatory pursuits, solely on the grounds of landing a sensational story. But not only was the matter dropped right there; in the postwar flurry of "war crimes" cases and the abortive trials of some specific instances, this incredible yarn emerging from the Balkans in March, 1916 never was mentioned in any of them.

It may be that in view of poison gas warfare having already been going on in the trench combat in northern France for almost a year by that time (since the end of April, 1915), the hundreds of thousands of soldiers who had already experienced this novelty in war weaponry greatly reduced the significance of this event involving presumably just 3,000 people. But there was a vast difference between the procedures and circumstances involved. Mass dispersal of cloud gas from cylinders along a broad geographical front depending on atmospherical dispersion had steadily resulted in fewer and fewer casualties as its targets learned to protect themselves by employing gas masks and other precautions; this atrocity case involved the charge that gas was used to kill people inside a closed building.

The above abbreviated account summarized by Professor Read which did get circulated in the West should have aroused a few dozen technical questions just among the curious, let along those who might have wanted to expand on this and go on to creating a vast and uniquely scandalous if not incendiary sensation. It would have been informative to know if this gassing operation had been repeated (the colossal figure of 700,000 massacred implied its repetition). Nothing was said as to which of the inhalant gases had been the agent and how much of it had to be used to saturate the premises from ceiling to floor in a large high-interior building such as an Eastern church (most gases *were* lighter than air), and how the church was made air-tight in the meantime. (How 3,000 people could have been kept passive if not inert long enough for this outlandish experiment to be inflicted upon them, a process which must have had to take quite a bit of time to be effective, wrinkles the brow. A group of 3,000 is sufficiently large enough to sponsor a substantial riot.) Nothing was known as to how and where the dead had been disposed of in Belgrade, and how the gas had been dispersed so as not to victimize the entire surrounding population including those who allegedly perpetrated this outrage. One can go on with such procedural queries at great length, each of which renders the yarn less credible, but the entire outlandish affair abruptly vanished, and nothing else of its nature was reported again.

38 The strangest case of a wartime book withdrawn by its publisher as a result of pressure of one kind or other was the acquiescence of the publisher Putnam, no small business, agreeing to take off the market their book *War, Peace and the Future,* by Ellen Key (1849-1926). (New York *Times,* May 31, 1918, p. 17.) But the pressure did not emanate from a branch of the Wilson government. It was applied by the National Security League, which was not a department of the Administration

or the armed forces. This organization was formed by a group of influential civilians in New York City on December 1, 1914 (New York *Times,* December 2, 1914, p. 1), 2-1/2 years before American entry into the European war. Its original purpose appeared to have been mainly to lobby in Washington to assist members of Congress working to increase military and naval spending and "Army and Navy Preparedness" (see note 15), as they announced upon their formation (a program deeply frowned on by President Wilson at that moment). Like their later-created analog, the American Defense Society, the NSL included several members deeply interested in the welfare of the arms and armament business. But their function took a far different course after April 6, 1917. Both organizations became involved in repeated interference in several civilian affairs in the country, and book-suppression was on the agenda of both.

NSL functionaries complained of Key's book because of the "unpatriotic sentiments" it contained. But the author was a *Swedish* civilian neutral, a world-famed feminist and author of a long string of books on many subjects, nearing 70 years of age and venerated at home as the "Pallas of Sweden." Her book had perhaps as much to do with women as with international statecraft (subtitled *A Consideration of Nationalism and Internationalism, and the Relation of Women to War*), and was written toward the end of 1914 and into 1915 in Swedish, for an obvious local audience. It was translated into English by Hildegard Norberg and issued by Putnam during American neutrality, in 1916. It was one of nearly a dozen books by Key which were available to American readers during the First World War era, and this one had received several reviews between 1916 and 1917, all kindly to commendatory. To expect American patriotism from a neutral woman years before the U.S.A. was even involved in the war undoubtedly was excessive, but it is likely the agitated people of the National Security League had not the faintest notion as to the identity of the author and the circumstances surrounding the coming into existence of the book in the first place.

[39] The tireless reiteration especially through the first two and a half years of World War One by the supporters of Britain's war party that they were at war with Germany because of what had happened to their buffer state Belgium soon had many echoes in North America. Helping out in forging the romantic imaginary portrait was the "gallant little Belgium" story of its alleged assistance in slowing down the German war machine's progress in the summer, 1914 campaign, a Thermopylæ-style epic narrative which really consisted almost entirely of fiction, as the entire account eventually became known. In a little over twenty years a new British war party was at war with Germany again, and the part played in bringing that about by two new buffer states, the Versailles-fabricated Poland and Czecho-Slovakia, has been described in a thousand accounts. Britain as the world's greatest buffer-state builder was described succinctly by Mary Barnes Gear in her March, 1941 article in the *Journal of Geography,* "The Role of Buffer States in International Relations." As a consequence of the war ending in 1945 it appears that the buffer state game in Europe is over for good, as the Continent has become a vast world backwater in the light of the dynamism of other parts of the globe. But in one geo-political sense and estimate one might describe the division of Europe between the Cold War adver-

saries ranged in the NATO and Warsaw Pact fronts as two vast agglomerations of buffer states separating the U.S.A. and U.S.S.R.

40 Naumann's book was read by many long after the war, though his proposal made no headway toward realization. The countries dominating the postwar settlements actually created several more new shaky and economically-unviable "states," making the problem between 1919 and 1939 much worse. Parker T. Moon in his formidable and frequently reprinted *Imperialism and World Politics* (New York: Macmillan, 1926), p. 458, considered Naumann an exponent of a new type or modification of Big Power imperialism, though it hardly represented in any particular what was then going on in Asia and Africa and the Pacific islands. When compared to the financial dragooning of the world's smaller nations in operation 60 years later, moreover, a subtle and sophisticated form of imperialism far exceeding anything ever known previously in the department of effective looting, Naumann's proposal was an essay in utter innocence. In a way Naumann was a precursor and anticipator of the American regional system of "continentalism" argued in the 1930s by Charles A. Beard, and the contemporary program for East Asia proposed by Japan, which was subjected to so much ridicule and hostility by fuglemen for the European (and American) colonial powers, and the related spokesmen and journalistic agents working for and looking forward to a non-Japanese-run Communist East Asia.

41 There is a specially puzzling and perhaps illogical aspect to the position of the Wilson War Government toward the publications and promotional activities of the pacifists and the Peace advocates generally. The continuous counter-propaganda which ceaselessly accused all elements involved of being a part of German propaganda efforts had an unwanted implication that only the German side desired the war to be brought to an end. The pacifists and Peace people had worked for the termination of the war beginning well before American formal involvement. Since labor in halting the war hardly could have much influence by insisting that only one side stop fighting, it is obvious that the Germans, by supporting at least in part the pacifist promotional material, were in harmony with the latter's idea of halting hostilities permanently, certainly by the half-way mark of the war, when it began to show signs to all of being a stalemate. On the other hand, the Anglo-French-American side, once a fact, did not back any peace program by any pacifist elements whatever. It created a problem for those trying to sort out the irreconcilable warriors from those willing to consider some kind of war settlement. Many expressed over the years deep mystification as to how Wilson as a neutral as late as the end of January, 1917 could have been so unequivocal in favor of a policy of ending the war without either side being the beneficiary, while emerging about nine weeks later as the unqualified paladin of the celestial importance of an unconditional triumph of "Allied" arms. Caught in the middle were the proponents of pacifism and peace of the previous 2-1/2 years, who now found themselves *ex post facto* an alleged sinister wing of the enemy's war aims and their pre-April, 1917 publications hunted and hounded as evil personified.

And for years after 1918, writers kept flailing away at some Germans for having supported and in part subsidized pacifist or peace printed materials as if it were a discredit all around. This is not too clearly established in some minds as correct, even if it suggests that the "Allies" were unconditionally behind the pursuit of a war course indefinitely and uninterested in a genuine peace alternative whatever, even when they were not doing well in martial enterprise (there has been for almost 75 years a special malevolence in the scorn and ridicule directed at the efforts of Henry Ford in seeking a peaceful end of the war in 1915, with perhaps the kindest estimate being that it was all a species of mild temporary insanity).

It may be that "there is no substitute for victory," but Americans and many others have many times accommodated themselves to far less than "victory" in the 160 or more wars of all kinds which have occurred since 1945. Many of these conflicts might never have happened if the forces generated by the consequences of "victory" after 1918 had never come into being. In the two-decades-long interim between the world wars, it was common to see remarks, especially by British writers, to the effect that American entry into the war in the spring of 1917 was a disaster for all Europe, and that had it not happened, peace would have been negotiated at about that time as a result of mutual exhaustion, to the great benefit and sustained well-being of everyone concerned and involved. An example of this was the remark by the well-known Storm Jameson on page 433 of her book *A Richer Dust* (New York: Knopf, 1931): "It would have been better if America had never come into the war, then no one would have won it and they would have made a decent peace."

An immense flap growing out of this subject occurred early in February, 1941 when the drive to involve the U.S.A. in the newest world war was under way, in which Winston Churchill, once more Prime Minister of Britain, was extremely active. The fireworks began to crackle when William Griffin in the February, 1941 issue of the magazine *Scribner's Commentator* ("When Churchill Said Keep Out," pp. 25-28) declared that Churchill in 1936 had also described American involvement in World War One an unlimited calamity for everyone. This was repeated by the celebrated liberal journalist and editor Oswald Garrison Villard, and also by one of the headlands in American literature in the first half of the twentieth century, Theodore Dreiser, in that same month. Dreiser's quotation of Churchill is as follows:

> America's entrance into the war was disastrous not only for your country but for the Allies as well, because had you stayed at home and minded your business we would have made peace with the Central Powers in the spring of 1917, and then there would have been no collapse in Russia, followed by Communism; no breakdown in Italy, followed by fascism; and Nazism would not at present be enthroned in Germany. If America had stayed out of the war and minded her own business, none of these isms would today be sweeping the continent of Europe and breaking down parliamentary government. (Dreiser, "This is Churchill's 'Democracy,'" *New Masses,* February 18, 1941, pp. 35-36.)

Villard's repetition of this just a few days earlier brought a repudiation from the British Embassy in Washington on February 12, 1941 (New York *Times,* February 13, 1941, p. 6). Embassy spokesmen cited Churchill as having denied ever having made such a declaration at any time, or any other statement having the same effect. But Porter Sargent, commenting on this eruption, quoted a well-known New England political commentator and writer, Beatrice Abbott, writing in the Boston *Transcript* newspaper, that if Churchill had not made any such pronouncement between the years 1919 and 1936, "he would probably be the only British writer who did not." And Sargent even found in the magazine *Unity* for January 20, 1941 a quotation of Churchill's son-in-law, Duncan Sandys, of this same sentiment expressed in 1939, a variant of which Churchill was now denying, almost two years later. (What impressed many was the length and detail of the statement attributed to Churchill, which the latter and his spokesmen were maintaining he had never uttered anywhere at any time.)

42 Snippets of the famed ceremonial bookburning in Germany in May, 1933 survive in various sources, and vary from trivial to nearly worthless. It becomes worse the more remote the account from the time of the event. And from the point of view of books and authors, the major emphasis here, what tends to survive as part of the historical record might just as well not be memorialized, since the errors, the omissions and the outright misinformation outweigh what little positive information is supplied. In the effort to make political points against those who initiated the action nearly everything of factual substance has been steadily sacrificed over the years.

Following the victory of the National Socialist Party in the German elections early in 1933 and the achievement of political control by this regime early in the spring of that year, a number of significant changes in policy occurred. One of them involved the repression by this regime of its various Marxist opponents, especially the German Communist Party, with whom they had fought in the streets for about a decade, as well as others who had an obvious intimate relation to the then-contemporary Bolshevik regime of Josef Stalin in Soviet Russia. But the offensive as it was to be reflected in the symbolic attack on literature, which dwelled on views, positions and attitudes which the NS regime considered hostile or inimical to its philosophy or its related policies and programs, extended to several other forces than Communists or related parties or groups, especially against what were construed as attacks on family institutions and the undermining of social stability and general traditional moral standards.

The New York *Times,* which printed a score of stories on the subject, some of them front-page-featured, in May 1933, divulged far more facts on the authors involved than the scant superficial accounts one may encounter today, and is much more reliable on the basic facts as well. It noted in April that this representative destruction of books by people it classified as adversaries was long planned, and the names of some of the authors were disclosed many days before the target date of May 10. Originally the *Times* reported that demonstrations were scheduled for 30 university towns, but through the third week of May, such book destructions were disclosed at only five. There was a separate bonfire before May 10 in Munich, and the one at the famed university in Heidelberg did not occur until May 18. And, since the *Times* condemned the action with strong words in three editorials in its issues of May 11, 12 and 13 it hardly can be lightly or superficially concluded that what it printed about the entire affair was intended to be diversionary or understated in any basic way.

If accounts one reads these days bother with geography they are likely to create the impression that this action took place only in Berlin. This was the largest of the reported events, organized by students of the University of Berlin, with undoubted assistance from the Ministry of Propaganda headed by Dr. Paul Josef Goebbels, the regimes's newly created secret police, and the backing of Captain Hermann Goering, a prominent figure in the government and a strong supporter of the anti-Communist aspect.

On the evening of May 10, on a fire built of crossed logs five feet high in Opera Square, students, preceded by a parade of 5,000 to the site, threw what was estimated as 20,000 copies of books, by about 45 designated authors, some of whom were identified vocally as the books were tossed in the flames. How many there actually were of both books and authors has been in dispute. The original list of the writers of Communist and other "un-German" works, as they were described on occasion, filled four typewritten pages and according to reporters totalled 160 writers (New York *Times,* May 6, 1933, p. 8), some of whom were journalists who had not written books. About 70% of these writers were obscure and never did get publicity. Only the authors with international reputations received much of any attention. The books had been gathered from public and school/university libraries, while some also came from raids on the private libraries of people the *Times* identified, without naming anyone, as "Marxist leaders." But it was emphasized that the private libraries and book collections of the citizenry at large were otherwise unmolested.

Eventually it was revealed about two weeks after the original bonfires were set that some 500 tons of "Marxist" books had been collected, but no one declared how many actually had been burned. In its story of May 22 the *Times* reported that there had been an extensive time-consuming sifting of this accumulation and that a large number were considered valuable and returned to libraries. Even the most notorious of the confiscated tomes were segregated in such a manner that 25 copies of each title were assigned to every government ministry and every university library for study "at some later time." So in one distinct impulse the program had gone quite contrary to destruction. In addition, German paper mills bid for this mass of literature, which included newspapers and magazines, accumulated in various cities, offering a price of a mark (then valued at 27.5 U.S. cents) per one hundred pounds. No one calculated how much of these sequestered books and other printed materials went to be pulped instead of burned. Their total market value in the opinion of the *Times* was very high, and there were suspicions that much of it might easily have been recycled back into private ownership instead of being pulped. As an operation almost entirely conducted by students, there were somewhat over-impulsive gestures made in gathering these books, and the *Times* on two occasions noted during the month that commissions of college professors had been appointed, largely at Captain Goering's insistence, which monitored the accumulations, and were responsible for the return of a substantial but undisclosed number of these books back to the libraries from which they had been taken. Nevertheless, Goering supported the event nationwide, and took credit for its anti-Communist objective, having declared at one point that after the campaign's major aim had been accomplished, "in fifty years nobody in Germany will know what Marxism is." (New York *Times,* May 22, 1933, p. 9).

Also enthusiastic over this demonstration was Dr. Goebbels, who affirmed what must have been obvious, its overall "symbolic significance" (New York *Times,* May 10, 1933, p. 1). For surely this ceremonial action could have resulted in the assemblage of only a tiny number of the millions of copies of these hundreds of works spread about Germany's seventy million people for more than three generations. Maybe no more than one-tenth of one per cent of the German populace participated in all these actions nationwide, and this mainly as spectators, if published figures on the onlookers were accurate. And it was observed by people visiting Germany in subsequent years that though the personnel of book stores were circumspect, the banned writers could be purchased almost anywhere from stocks kept "under the counter."

As to student book burnings held elsewhere than Berlin, those at the University of Munich in their demonstration were calculated to have burned about 100 books. Those at Frankfurt-am-Main also burned "Marxist" and "un-German" books, as reported, but no estimate was made as to number. The student participators at the University of Breslau were supposed to have torched 5,000 *pounds* of books, while participating students at the University of Kiel were estimated to have consigned 2,000 copies of the targeted volumes to their bonfire. The *Times* reported that a preliminary or maybe premature burning of what was described as "Marxist literature" took place in Munich May 9 while an estimated audience of 5,000 school children watched, the only such reported demonstration not consisting primarily of university students. The tardiest of the incendiary shows reported was that at the University of Heidelberg. A large pile of books estimated at "several thousand" were burned on the campus, after first being "covered with Communist flags." The *Times* story (May 19, 1933, p. 9) related that the students cheered while the blaze consumed the books.

Concerning the banned authors, about 50 of the 160 on the master list were identified in spring, 1933 newspaper accounts, and eventually received public notice. About three fourths of these persons had substantial reputations and were of German birth or citizenship, including a virtual pantheon of those with lengthy Marxist or Communist pedigrees. The remainder were mostly Soviet Russians and a scattering of Americans; only two were women. And only four book titles were specifically named in all the *Times* reportage. The assumption was however that the entire output of the cited writers was under formal ban, or official displeasure.

Analyzed in another way, it was impossible to escape the generational nature, which more and more took on the cast of an operation in which the young were repudiating or destroying the work of the dead or the old. Of the 51 writers mentioned by name in dispatches from Germany in the *Times* during the month of May 1933, only three were born in the 20th century. One third were already deceased, only five had been born after 1890, only 14 after 1880. And the average age of the still living authors on this list was over 55.

Contemporary commentary on the origins of the idea which ended in the ceremonial bookburnings of May 10, 1933 indicates that it took shape at least eight weeks before the event and probably some time before that, with the promotion of the program and the first gathering of books getting attention at least a month before. We find speculation at that time that it all was originally a publicity-seeking adventure conceived by members of the Deutsche Studentenschaft (New York *Times,* April 13, 1933, p. 8), which group eventually bore the burden of executing the actions in the various university towns. However, in view of the attention this demonstration was to get, worldwide, and the lasting impact resulting from the endless repetition of the story in the succeeding two generations, the German students in 1933 were to derive vastly more publicity in historical residue than they possibly could ever have expected, let alone bargained for. As an agency for book-destruction it all was of minor significance; as an exploited symbol it still has no equal.

43 Cerf, "War and the Book Business," *Publishers Weekly* (March 28, 1942), p. 1248.

Among the moguls of the publishing industry who shared with Cerf the dominance in wartime book control as vested in the Council on Books in Wartime was Cass Canfield, head of the ancient and prestigious house of Harper starting in 1932. And Canfield had some experience in the action described by Cerf, junking books with an uncomfortable political stance and absorbing the loss, even before the U.S.A. was a World War Two belligerent.

In the spring of 1940 Harper was about to bring out a book by an author they had twice published previously, Lawrence Dennis, a colorful public figure with an already substantial career in the diplomatic, financial, literary and ideological worlds. Dennis' new volume, *The Dynamics of War and Revolution,* was already bound in cloth with the Harper imprint and jacket when the spectacular collapse of France and Britain took place in their war with the Germans in May-June, 1940, one of the most dismaying and heartrending events in world history to American Francophiles and Anglophiles of the American East Coast. The horror which Dennis' book, with its bleak and drastic criticism of these just-defeated lands and their between-the-wars regimes, might further cause to the sensibilities of their grievously wounded partisans here, impelled Canfield to cancel abruptly all plans to distribute it.

A tiny handful of copies managed to get loose but that was all; the edition was almost totally destroyed. But Dennis managed to obtain some of the bound copies and had them recovered and issued under the imprint of his provocative newsletter devoted mainly to world politics, *Weekly Foreign Letter.* Despite Harper's repudiation and destruction the book became a celebrated under-ground item for decades, gaining adherents and readers. Copies began to command premium out-of-print prices shortly after the demise of Dennis in 1977 and it was reprinted by the Institute for Historical Review in California in 1980, only to become a victim of still a new suppression in the form of the total destruction of the new edition in the arson fire which swept the premises of the Institute on July 4, 1984.

44 Cerf, "War and the Book Business," *above,* p. 1249. About the only criticism this staggering proposal by Cerf received came from William Henry Chamberlin, who predicted that it would make Americans "dependent for our knowledge of

Russia on straight Communist propaganda," and provide an unimaginable blow to "impartial knowledge and judgment." Chamberlin, letter to editors of *The Christian Century* (August 19, 1942), p. 1008.

Chamberlin knew perfectly well what Cerf was doing, and trying to achieve strategically, but in view of the climate of the times chose not to explicate. Cerf, and the powerful and affluent forces he represented, almost totally devoid of anyone even remotely attached to the Communist Party and for that matter largely uninvolved with the Soviet Union or any of its people, had not the faintest intention to sell Communist propaganda or to make America receptive in the long run to Communist rhetoric and ideology or to set it up in the distant future for a Communist takeover. As it was waggishly remarked, the U.S.A. might have "gone cannibal" well before it might have "gone Communist." What the formidable interests Cerf and his fellow publisher potentates represented were determined to do was to stifle or suffocate any wartime criticism of Stalinist *foreign policy,* especially in Europe, the superficial reason for this being that such criticism might play a part in "losing" the war. Squelching or pulping books written by critics or traditional antagonists of Stalinist ambitions, particularly in Europe, was indeed a formidable psychological and ideological assist, directly or indirectly, and whether it all led to a maximum portion of Continental Europe coming under Soviet domination as part of a gigantic Red empire or consisting on its edges of countries with genial attitudes toward Stalinist or sovietized neighbors, did not bother Cerf and his circle at all; they never appeared to oppose such a possibility or express concern over such a likelihood.

That this had resulted before the famed summit conferences of 1945 took place, at which latter the "betrayal" of "democracy" allegedly occurred, can be established easily by a sustained examination of mass communication outside the U.S.S.R. in the 1941-1944 period. It all transpired with just a faint expression of contemporary protest, the latter being subjected to withering ridicule while the Red Army legions rolled across Europe. It may be argued that discussion thousands of miles from where it was all happening might not have made much difference anyway, though failure to cooperate with it without some conditions while it was going on, by the wartime U.S.A. and British regimes, would certainly have resulted in a Europe looking far different from what it does and has for over forty years.

It took a special kind of Anglo-American Establishment mind to believe that many billions could be poured into making the Soviet armed forces triumphant and ominously threatening, but that they could be talked out of all the real estate such power had permitted them to occupy, by some simple-minded moralistic palaver at a political conference somewhere. When the formal sniveling had subsided upon the swift bursting of this preposterous balloon of wishful thinking there followed shortly after a new semi-lunacy, the policy of "containment," which distracted the busy for years but managed only to freeze the fluidity of 1945 into a new and just as dangerous status quo ("containment" managed to achieve very little in Asia and almost nothing in Africa). But one may suggest that deep down, no one expected any significant change to occur as a result of the likes of Yalta and Potsdam, anyway.

Preceding "containment" abroad by a brief interval was the beginning of a synthetic crusade at home, especially in North America. In the decade of 1946-1956, roughly, a theatric "anti-Communist" investigation under multiple auspices saturated public attention, and while turgid ham-acting took place connected with annoying Stalinist-sympathizing clerks, dentists and writers of lightweight movie scripts intended for viewers in the lower third of the intelligence quotient range, this very important aspect of the previous selling of World Communist foreign policy did not enter the agenda at all; it had all been part of "winning the war," one was supposed to understand. Thus while American show-biz staging was applied to grandiose topics such as whether pro-Soviet writers of mystery stories and Broadway plays subtly smuggled Marxist messages into their yarns and products subliminally, twelve countries of Europe went under Stalinist domination; Red gunfire, not Communists in the U.S. State Department, took China, much of Korea and almost all of Southeast Asia into a companion form of Communism. The colonial systems in Asia and Africa collapsed spectacularly, allowing the possibility of scores more of such inroads, and the state was set for decades more of the same kind of international political developments. This was the real fruit of Cerf's call to make publishing or selling of books even mildly critical of "our gallant Soviet ally" either disrespectable or punishable, but preferably impossible.

The accompaniment of the Communist "subversion" search-and-destroy mission, where it was inoperable or insignificant, was an impressive new "anti-Communist" growth-industry, which sought with some success to inculcate terror of a system which could not even feed itself, seemed to have much trouble making a door correctly, produced automobiles 20 years behind the state of the art, and whose color television sets were still exploding frequently in the living rooms of citizens all over the Soviet Union over forty years later. But, for those of the "West" with very long range strategic visions and who had better understanding as to why wars are fought than to kill Bad Ideas, the replacement of the fierce industrial, trade and financial competition of the system headed in Europe by Germany by the creaking incompetence of the U.S.S.R., and the similar formidability in the Far East represented by Japan replaced by a Red China that chose to go back two centuries, was not all a negative balance sheet.

[45] *Publishers Weekly* (September 5, 1942), p. 833.

[46] The history of author and book suppression in Asia is a prodigious one, and could be worked into an encyclopædia-sized set of works, in its entirety. A brief and incidental effort to bring the subject down to date in one very limited region for a very short period of time might be made here as a fragmentary illustration. In July, 1988 there was the beginning of a policy of rehabilitating in South Korea some 125 authors who had fled to North Korea during roughly the years of warfare between the two, 1950-1953. Their works had been banned by the regime based in Seoul up to this time. The situation in China covering this subject over the last 40 years probably cannot even be imagined; undoubtedly both the Peking (Beijing) and Taipei regimes have prodigious lists of banned books and writers.

Appendix

A Beginner's Manual for Apprentice Book Burners

A Preliminary Reading List
of books dealing with minority opinions, unorthodox or unpopular viewpoints, and other unpleasant subjects, as well as a number of unusual topics and out-of-the-ordinary interpretations in several fields of learning, with some aggravating standard works which have survived decades of smearing included here and there.

Author's Note 1988:The annotated bibliography here republished originally appeared in The Amateur Book Collector, *Volume V, Number 4 (December, 1954). It was an outgrowth of a mimeographed version given out every spring to graduating students majoring in the social studies, intended to encourage intellectual curiosity and a continuing interest in growth and understanding in ideological and intellectual subjects of many kinds. The title was whimsical, of course, and was not intended to suggest that the entries in the listing had in fact been banned or suppressed anywhere. But most of the works had drawn extreme criticism in many circles of one kind or another in many places over the years, and might easily have been candidates for suppression or interdiction given proper incitatory events. They were actual reading experiences of the writer, who never heard a single one of them ever mentioned in a formal class in seventeen years of formal education, and were entirely a product of extracurricular browsing in a wide variety of libraries, book collections and book stores. Were it brought up to date it would of course be much larger, but this would distort the historical aspect of the exercise, and constitute a substantial deviation from the original intent and objective. It might be added also in passing that after 35 years a number of these controversial works have become what might be described as "standards" of a sort, and may have lost the aura of controversy they enjoyed at the various times they were first encountered and read. In republishing this original piece the intention is primarily bibliographical, an assist of sorts to younger contemporaries who might be interested in learning of these works and thus induced to search out copies for their personal libraries. It also serves incidentally to document the writer's long-standing interest in controversial literature, an example of which is the primary work at hand.*

The original bibliographical article is reproduced precisely as it was originally published, without cuts, additions, alterations, or subsequent glosses or commentaries of any kind. The intent is not only to present a useful bibliographical tool but to preserve its historical significance as a way things were looked at over a generation ago.

An Inadequate Preface

HISTORY is a science of reasoning *based solely on evidence* consisting of documents, *to which critical intelligence has been applied.* Without documents there can be no detailed grasp of the past, and anything written without a foundation on documents cannot properly be called history. Factual evidence based on documents is acquired and observed under conditions where a variable area of the unknown is an ingredient. Therefore, the historical method must combine the knowledge of the particular conditions under which the facts of the past incident in question occurred with an understanding of the general conditions under which the facts of humanity occur.

There has yet to be a study of any human society by anybody who escaped his biases, no matter how he struggled to attain impartiality. Any writer of history, especially, must face the fact that he can not evade the cultural and social determinants of his theories, ideas, religion, nationality, social and economic position, and his various conscious and unconscious affinities with assorted individuals and classes, as well as the powerful influences emanating from his own historical environment. At all times there is a constant deviation ranging from conscious distortion on one hand to *unconscious distortion* on the other, which latter often occurs at the very time when the writer feels most impartial of all. *There has yet to appear a satisfactory remedy for this state of affairs. In other words, we all still write within the confines of some "frame of reference."*

Those who write in the related "social science" fields are certainly no exceptions to the above observations; bias and distortion in the productions of economists, sociologists, political scientists, psychologists and anthropologists compare quite favorably with that of which the historians are guilty. Consequently, it behooves students to approach with great caution works which make obvious claims to impartiality and "objectivity." There are serious doubts as to the applicability of such terminology. One must beware of the label "objective" in particular ; *the prevailing tendency is to apply this "approval" word to viewpoints which are mainly the consensus of the most generally held conventional attitudes and sentiments.* This is one of the most widely prevalent semantic diseases afflicting the people who live in our time, and the temptation to engage in this practice is almost irresistible. It further accounts, in part, for the sharp decline in discussion and debate upon, and the panic-stricken avoidance of, anything which gets tagged "controversial." Nothing could be more deplorable in a society which makes such protestations of being open and "free."

One remedy for "objectiv-itis," admittedly imperfect, consists of reading the literature of the unorthodox or unpopular viewpoint on as many subjects as possible, instead of consuming the titles of books and the opinions of those who have read them. It is one of the few avenues leading to the development of an intelligent critical facility. In the process, one must not be dissuaded by threats of becoming "biased," or exhortations not to become a "de-bunker." That "debunking" is unpopular and "de-bunkers" are shunned is simply testimony to the existence of an immense appetite and audience for "bunk." Once we sink to the position where reverence for some official version inhibits further investigation and revision of the account of any area of the human past, history and the social studies will have

111

attained the level now occupied by astrology.

This list is an experimental effort, and is intended for students of history and the allied social studies, in the hope of modifying in some degree the tendencies toward smugness and condescension which are partially acquired from extended contact with the academic approach. It is quite possible that a thousand such lists could be prepared, all of them superior to this one. The only significance this one possesses is that the books contained in it are drawn from my own reading experiences.

Partly for the Bibliographical Record:

Do you think that "book-burning" in either its figurative or literal sense was invented by persons outside "the Anglo-Saxon tradition," which is usually portrayed as one of tolerance and respect for civil rights? Have you the impression that people in this country have behaved fundamentally differently from those of other lands during periods of stress, panic and crisis, in matters dealing with unpopular thinking, or spoken or written unorthodoxy? On the contrary, the following titles are a small sample of the enormous literature dealing with suppression, censorship, destruction and other forms of violence and interference with freedom of expression in England and the United States, starting as far back as the 17th century.

Gillett, Charles Ripley. *Burned Books: Neglected Chapters in British History and Literature.* 2 vols. New York: Columbia Univ. Press, 1932. The author was librarian emeritus of Union Theological Seminary. 723 pages total, of inestimable value to students of the free speech struggle, especially in matters of religious conviction.

Haight, Anne Lyon. *Banned Books: Informal Notes on Some Books Banned for Various Reasons at Various Times and in Various Places.* New York: R.R. Bowker Co., 1935.

Schroeder, Theodore. *Free Speech Bibliography.* New York: H.W. Wilson Co., 1922.

Rosenthal, Clarice A., Meeker, M., Ottenberg, M., and Others. *Selected Bibliography on Civil Liberties in the United States.* New York: American Civil Liberties Union, 1937. First published December 1937. There is a mimeographed supplement to this which was issued under ACLU auspices dated June 1939.

Seldes, George. *You Can't Print That!* New York: Harcourt, 1929. *Freedom of the Press.* Indianapolis: Bobbs-Merrill, 1935. *You Can't Do That.* New York: Modern Age Books, 1938. *Tell The Truth and Run.* New York: Greenberg, 1953.

Bradbury, Ray. *Fahrenheit 451.* New York: Ballantine Books, 1953.

Have you been doped with "adjustment" psychology and psychiatric theory? Do you think that all non-conformists and alleged "neurotic" and "maladjusted" folk need to be brought to "normal" patterns of behaving? Read the volume below: the author has some different ideas. In this connection as well, consult David Karp's *One,* mentioned below.

Lindner, Robert. *Prescription for Rebellion.* New York: Rinehart, 1952.

Are you under the influence of the school of thought that conceives technology as a one way street to unlimited opulence and ease. Do you think there is no dark side to machine age gadgetry? Are you under the illusion that continual technological revolution is producing no crisis in the economic and social value systems we take for granted as originating from on high? Maybe Wiener and Juenger will alter your optimism. Finish up with Kurt Vonegut, Jr.'s novel *Player Piano.* New York: Scribners, 1953. Wiener, Norbert. *Cybernetics.* New York: John Wiley, 1947. *The Human Use of Human Beings.* New York: John Wiley, 1951.

Juenger, Friedrich Georg. *The Failure of Technology: Perfection Without Purpose.* Chicago: Regnery, 1949.

Are you sure there is no case against humanitarianism, humility, meekness, benevolence and allied values? Read Redbeard: those who adhere to the Sermon on the Mount or the Golden Rule should be among the first to want this volume burned.

Redbeard, Ragnar. *Might is Right.* London: W.J. Robbins, 1910; Chicago: Dill Pickle Press, 1927.

Do you know anything about anthropology? Here are three most engaging and controversial books, in that area. White and Dorsey ought to get you mad and keep you that way for awhile. Day is in a class all by himself in the readability department.

Dorsey, George. *Man's Own Show: Civilization.* New York: Harper, 1931.

White, Leslie A. *The Science of Culture.* New York: Farrar and Straus, 1949.

Day, Clarence. *This Simian World.* New York: Knopf, 1936.

Two classic criticisms of the structure and value system of the American Way of Life. You will not find either distributed at the luncheons of "service" organizations in your town.

Veblen, Thorstein. *The Theory of the Leisure Class.* Several editions. Modern Library (1934) and another pocket book edition (1953) among several since 1899.

Mills, C. Wright. *White Collar: The American Middle Classes.* New York: Oxford Univ. Press, 1951.

Do you think all the English pull their punches like Churchill when needling the U.S.A.? Mr. Wayman's blast is an example of what we rarely ever see here.

Wayman, Leonard. *Moonshine America.* London: Golden Galley Press, 1948. As a counterweight, for Anglophiles and assorted lovers of our British "betters," try swallowing Robert Briffault's *The Decline and Fall of the British Empire.* New York: Simon and Schuster, 1938.

Orators usually maintain a deep silence concerning much of the content of the following titles on February 12. No "objective" Lincoln student should be caught with any of them around the house in any spot except in the fireplace.

Horton, Rushmore G. *A Youth's History of the Great Civil War.* Rev. ed., Dallas: Southern Publishing Co., 1925.

Minor, Charles L.C. *The Real Lincoln: From the Testimony of his Contemporaries.* 4th edition, Gastonia, N.C.: Atkins-Rankin Co., 1928.

Manigault, G. *The United States Unmasked*. London: Edward Stanford, 1879. This one was so bitter toward the Union that he couldn't get a publisher in the U.S.A.

Coggins, James C. *Abraham Lincoln, A North Carolinian*. Asheville, N.C.: Advocate Pub. Co., 1925; 2nd edition, Atkins-Rankin Co. (Gastonia), 1928.

Has everybody succumbed to industrialism and urbanism? There is no longer the possibility of stating the case of pre- Civil War Southern-style agrarianism? Wait until you examine the next title, about the most bothersome reappearance of this argument in the 20th century. Every good book bonfire should have one.

Twelve Southerners. *I'll Take My Stand: The South and the Agrarian Tradition*. New York: Harper, 1930.

Did it ever dawn on you that our ancestors were often subject to the same failings and sins we deplore about us today? The following volumes are part of a large literature telling us of their "this-worldly interests."

Washburn, R.C. *Prayer for Profit*. New York: Sears, 1930.

Sakolski, Aaron. *The Great American Land Bubble*. New York: Harper, 1932.

Loth, David. *Public Plunder: A History of Graft in America*. New York: Carrick and Evans, 1936.

Herbert Asbury discusses their drinking habits with great charm in *The Great Illusion* (New York: Doubleday, 1950). You might also read Asbury's great short story "Hatrack," which appeared first in the April, 1926 *American Mercury,* and was reprinted in the November, 1950 issue of the same journal. It was suppressed the first time it came out and the *Mercury* temporarily lost its mailing privilege, because of it.

Have you read George Orwell's *Nineteen Eighty-Four?* You might profit from another reading. then follow it with the Pohl-Kornbluth and Karp entries below; all three are in the best tradition of top rate modern science fiction.

Orwell, George. *Nineteen Eighty-Four*. London: Secker & Warburg, 1949; New York: Harcourt, 1949. Also a pocket book paperback issue.

Pohl, Frederik, and Kornbluth, C.M. *The Space Merchants*. New York: Ballantine Books, 1953.

Karp, David. *One*. New York: Vanguard, 1953.

Are you an advocate of the Toynbee approach to the philosophy of history? The two books below are a most unpleasant counter-agent.

Spengler, Oswald. *The Decline of the West*. One volume edition, New York: Knopf, 1937.

Adams, Brooks. *The Law of Civilization and Decay*. New edition, New York: Knopf, 1943.

The following title should be read in conjunction with *Gulliver's Travels,* and is easily the most clever satirical political writing since the former appeared.

Orwell, George. *Animal Farm*. London: Secker & Warburg, 1949; other editions elsewhere and earlier.

The shady side of the American business system is a topic of interest only to communist authors? Its weaknesses all myths dreamed up by the gremlins in the Kremlin? Here is a brief but potent sample to contradict this; there is a vast list of others of this kind. It could be supplemented with E.H. Sutherland, *White Collar Crime*. New York: Dryden Press, 1948.

Flynn, John T. *Graft in Business*. New York: Vanguard, 1931. *Security Speculation*. New York: Harcourt, 1934.

Ernst, Morris. *Too Big*. Boston: Little, Brown, 1940.

Quinn, Theodore K. *Giant Business: Threat to Democracy; The Autobiography of an Insider*. New York: Exposition Press, 1953.

Radicals are all saints? Or are they all monsters? Nomad's two books are immensely readable and take up both these stands in a manner that deserves some extra attention.

Nomad, Max. *Rebels and Renegades*. New York: Macmillan, 1932. *Apostles of Revolution*. Boston: Little, Brown, 1939.

Do you think all scientists are laboratory-bound, unimaginative souls who know nothing outside the world of test-tubes? Zinsser ought to demolish that notion. You could also try the "medical biographies" by the physician Charles Maclaurin, *Post Mortem* and *Mere Mortals* (New York: Doran, 1923, 1925).

Zinsser, Hans. *Rats, Lice and History*. Boston: Little, Brown, 1935. Some pocket book editions.

A memorable piece of fictional writing dealing with the struggle of simple people against reaction:

Silone, Ignazio. *Fontamara*. New York: Harrison Smith, 1934; another edition, Modern Age, 1938.

Two books about the Far East which lack the condescending missionary tone:

Patric, John. *Yankee Hobo in the Orient*. 7th ed., Frying Pan Creek, Oregon: John Patric, 1945.

Michener, James. *The Voice of Asia*. New York: Random House, 1951.

Lose your religious friends rapidly by quoting portions of these books to them:

Robertson, John Mackinnon. *The Jesus Myth; Pagan Christs*.

McCabe, Joseph. *The Story of Religious Controversy*. Boston: Stratford, 1929.

Mencken, Henry L. *Treatise on the Gods*. New York: Knopf, 1930.

Blanshard, Paul. *American Freedom and Catholic Power*. Boston: Beacon, 1950.

Foote, G.W., and Ball, W.P. *The Bible Handbook*. 10th ed., London: The Pioneer Press, 1953.

Doane, Thomas W. *Bible Myths and Their Parallels in Other Religions*. New York: J.W. Bouton, 1883.

Did you ever wonder what motivated people to believe in an join mass movements? Are totalitarian shirts interchangeable? Hoffer is unique in the theory department; you might follow it up by checking up on any number of re-tread believers; Valtin is one of the most typical.

Hoffer, Eric. *The True Believer: Thoughts on the Nature of Mass Movements*. New York: Harper, 1951.

Valtin, Jan. *Out of the Night*. New York: Alliance, 1941.

Five wonderful books by George Orwell of varied controversial nature; study modern writing style from a master.

Orwell, George. *Down and Out in Paris and London*. New York: Harper, 1933; several other editions. *Homage to Catalonia*. London: Secker & Warburg, 1938; New York: Harcourt, 1952. *Coming up for Air*. London: Gollancz, 1939; Secker & Warburg, 1945; elsewhere as well. *Shooting an Elephant and Other Essays*. New York: Harcourt, 1950. *Dickens, Dali and Other Essays*. New York: Reynal, 1946.

Would you like to be called a reactionary by your friends in professional education? Tell them you read these:

Smith, Mortimer. *And Madly Teach*. Chicago: Henry Regnery, 1949.

Lynd, Robert. *Quackery in the Public Schools*. Boston: Little, Brown, 1953.

Bestor, Arthur E., Jr. *Educational Wastelands: The Retreat From Learning in our Public Schools*. Urbana: University of Illinois Press, 1953.

Smith, Mortimer. *The Diminished Mind: A Study of Planned Mediocrity in Our Public Schools*. Chicago: Henry Regnery, 1954.

My three favorite autobiographies:

Adams, Henry. *The Education of Henry Adams*. New York: Houghton Mifflin, 1918; other editions.

Goldman, Emma. *Living My Life*. One volume edition; New York: Knopf, 1934.

Nock, Albert Jay. *Memoirs of a Superfluous Man*. New York: Harper, 1943.

For those who think capital punishment is the ultimate in criminology, and for the simple folk who have equated the courts, the law, the judges and the lawyers with justice:

Duff, Charles. *A Handbook of Hanging*. London: John Lane, The

Bodley Head, 1928, 1938, 1954.

Kropotkin, Peter. *Organized Vengeance Called Justice.* London: Freedom Press has released several editions and printings since it first appeared in 1902.

Rodell, Fred. *Woe Unto You Lawyers!* New York: Reynal, 1939.

Two of the most irritating books ever written by Henry L. Mencken, a great controversialist:

Mencken, Henry L. *In Defense of Women.* New York: Knopf, 1922; Garden City, 1931. *Notes on Democracy.* New York: Knopf, 1926.

Conscientious objectors to war make good hate subjects. What do you know of their side of the story? The next two items are just a fragment of a copious literature:

Cantine, Holley, and Rainer, Dachine. *Prison Etiquette.* Bearsville, New York: Retort Press, 1950.

Naeve, Lowell. *Fields of Broken Stones.* (In collaboration with David Wieck.) Glen Gardner, New Jersey: Libertarian Press, 1950.

Hennacy, Ammon. *Autobiography of a Catholic Anarchist.* New York: The Catholic Worker, 1954.

A most interesting psychological study of our "blood and guts" best-sellers and comic books, and some remarks on the persons who manufacture them. A much-frowned-upon book, and one that is not going to be obtained without considerable effort:

Legman, G. *Love and Death.* New York: Privately printed, 1949.

Two good books for students of American History, quite different in subject and structure, one long established, the other not too well known, and both worth burning:

Beard, Charles A. *An Economic Interpretation of the Constitution.* Various editions and printings since 1913; try New York: Macmillan, 1948.

Hofstadter, Richard. *The American Political Tradition and the Men Who Made It.* New York: Knopf, 1948.

A much quoted critique of political democracy, USA style, by an "outlander," deserves a wider audience despite its age:

Ostrogorski, M. *Democracy and the Party System in the United States*. New York: Macmillan, 1910. Other editions.

By now you have probably internationalized the value system of mass culture sufficiently to hate all the following authors:

Hello, Ernest. *The Mediocre Man.*

Faguet, Emile. *The Cult of Incompetence* (Beatrice Barstow, trans.). New York: Dutton, 1912.

Ortega y Gasset, Jose. *The Revolt of the Masses*. New York: Norton, 1932; also Pocket Books, 1950.

Campbell, Francis Stuart. *The Menace of the Herd*. Milwaukee: Sheed and Ward, 1943.

A most absorbing introduction to the IWW, if you have never heard of them or in case you have already acquired someone else's prejudices toward them:

Chaplin, Ralph. *Wobbly*. Chicago: University of Chicago Press, 1948.

No doubt the name "Machiavelli," if it means anything to you, has acquired a connotation of sinister and evil things; the emotional engineering aimed at producing this effect must have succeeded by now. Why not take a crack at him anyway; then try Burnham's book and then the primary items of the men he mentions. The total equals a first rate political education.

Machiavelli, Nicolo. *The Prince*. Several editions; a recent Pocket Book edition.

Burnham, James. *The Machiavellians: Defenders of Freedom*. New York: John Day, 1943.

Michels, Robert. *Political Parties: A Sociological Study of the Oligarchical Tendencies in Modern Democracy*. New York: Hearst International Press, 1915; Glencoe, Illinois: Free Press, 1949.

de Grazia, Alfred (editor & translator). *Roberto Michels' First Lectures in Political Sociology*. Minneapolis: University of Minnesota Press, 1949.

Sorel, Georges. *Reflections on Violence*. Several editions; latest: Glencoe, Illinois: Free Press, 1949.

Mosca, Gaetano. *The Ruling Classes*. New York: McGraw Hill, 1939.

Pareto, Vilfredo. *The Mind and Society* (Arthur Livingston, translator). 4 vols. New York: Harcourt, 1935. Try vols. 1 and 2; the whole set is an immense task.

It is customary to deprecate the "amateur" trying his hand in any field; the "scientific" economists are especially adept at this strategem. But there is no field of learning in which there is such a lack of an accepted body of truth, such an absence of consensus of authority, or of persons who can be mentioned without question as to their reliability, as economics. Despite the smears, some of the "amateurs" have done worthy work. One of the most substantial is George; follow it up with Bilgram and Levy. They are unorthodox but hard to squelch:

George, Henry. *Progress and Poverty*. Several editions since 1879; a current one sponsored by the Robert Schalkenbach Foundation, New York City.

Bilgram, Hugo, and Levy, L.E. *The Cause of Business Depressions*. Philadelphia: Lipincott, 1914.

One of the most vaguely treated matters in political theory is the origin of the institution called the "state." Try the four below for another approach in the contemporary "great debate" on the subject, which manages to stay five light years away from the issues:

Nock, Albert Jay. *Our Enemy the State*. Caldwell, Idaho: Caxton Printers, 1946. (Re-edition.)

Oppenheimer, Franz. *The State*. New York: Vanguard, 1928. Other editions and publishers.

Bakunin, Michael. *God and the State*. Several editions since 1881; a recent one by Modern Publishers, Indore, India, 1946.

Bourne, Randolph. *The State*. To be found in several places; an excellent pamphlet edition by Resistance Press, New York City, 1946-1947.

In playing the modern game of politics, one should pay careful attention to the revisions in the rules, which have been especially streamlined since totalitarian faiths have perfected their advertising departments. It is now customary for all fervid political believers to refuse to credit rival believers with even the most elementary traits of honesty; all contrary ideologies are always sinister and mendacious, and of course this stigma carries over to those expounding same. In training for posts as book-burners, with a specialty in ideological material, it is becoming very difficult to acquire competence without a knowledge of just what should be burned, and exactly *why*. This crisis, accordingly, is forcing us back to a most "reactionary" position: we are being pressed to the edge of the precipice, so to speak, and forced, in our desperation, *to try to understand what each evil and loathsome doctrine is by reading the explanation of it emanating from the group that propounds it*. This, of course, is a most startling and vicious recommendation. It undermines our growing dependence on slick manuals prepared by various ideologues who pretend unsurpassed "objectivity" and fairness exceeding all comprehension, and who succeed in palming off Procrustean summaries of all the "Isms" except the particular swamproot they imbibe. And of course it veritably undermines the American Way by questioning the validity of subscribing to a newspaper or journal, and taking one's definitions as prepared, canned at the editor's table. Surely it is a grave breach of intellectual etiquette to suggest that one cannot get a careful explanation of Communism in the *Chicago Tribune, The New Leader,* the *American Mercury* and *Time,* nor a suitable definition of Fascism in *The New Republic, The Nation, Harper's* and the *Daily Worker.* But let us dally a bit, and in a fit of sheer romantic delusion, indulge in such preposterous presumptions as alluded to above.

In the mixed category below, a pretty fair presentation of the Fascist outlook is that of Palmieri. For National Socialism, which is not the same, one should read Hitler and find out what he actually had to say. Then follow up with a critic of the unhysterical sort; Rauschning is representative. Did you absorb the William L. Shirer -type hysteria? Was there nothing to National Socialism to attract such vast support? Read Kneller. the sources of the opposition can be explored in Rothfels, especially. (Excellent stuff of source type are the von Hassell

Diaries and Hans Gisevius, *To the Bitter End* [Boston, 1947].) If you
have gotten Karl Marx at second hand all your life, it is time to read
him and try to make sense out of Marxism yourself for a change. You
could consult some of the other principal prophets of Communism as
well; they write with considerable more clarity than Marx. The best
bibliographies of books on Soviet Russia have not appeared in the
Readers' Digest or the *Daily Worker;* the spring issue, 1948, of the
now defunct magazine *Politics* and the fall, 1953 issue of the *Anvil
and Student Partisan* combined are pretty formidable. Rosenberg's
history is one of the best:

Palmieri, Mario. *The Philosophy of Fascism.* Chicago: Dante
Alighieri Society, 1936.

Hitler, Adolf. *Mein Kampf (My Battle).* Many editions; try New
York: Houghton, 1939.

Rauschning, Herman. *The Revolution of Nihilism: Warning to the
West.* New York: Longmans, 1939.

Rauschning, Herman. *Voice of Destruction: Hitler Speaks.* London: Butterworth, 1939. New York: Putnam, (1940).

Kneller, George F. *The Educational Philosophy of National
Socialism.* New Haven: Yale, 1941.

Rothfels, Hans. *The German Opposition to Hitler.* Chicago: Henry
Regnery, 1948.

Marx, Karl. *The Manifesto of the Communist Party.* New York:
International Publishers, 1937.

Marx, Karl. *Capital.* New York: Charles H. Kerr Co., 1906; also a
Modern Library edition.

Lenin, V.I. *What Is To Be Done?* Vol. 4 of *Selected Works.* New
York: International Publishers, 1929.

Werner, M.R. *Stalin's Kampf.* (Selection of Stalin's writings.) New
York: Howell, Soskin, 1940.

Trotsky, Leon. *The Revolution Betrayed.* New York: Doubleday,
1937.

Rosenberg, Arthur. *A History of Bolshevism from Marx to the
Five Year Plan.* New York: Oxford, 1935.

It has become unfashionable to study anarchism, "the conscience
of the left." Even the left and the liberals prefer to ignore it as they

devote themselves to more "practical" faiths. Here is a stripped-down list of "musts" for the understanding of the various theories; it should be preceded by a reading of Kropotkin's article in the *Encyclopædia Britannica*. The bibliography of anarchist writings runs to at least ten thousand entries.

In Europe:

Proudhon, P.J. *System of Economical Contradictions, or the Philosophy of Misery*. Boston: Tucker, 1888.

Proudhon, P.J. *What is Property?* (B. R. Tucker, translator.) New York: Humboldt Pub. Co., no date.

Proudhon, P.J. *General Idea of the Revolution in the Nineteenth Century*. (J.B. Robinson, translator.) London: Freedom Press, 1923.

Maximov, G. P., translator. *Political Philosophy of Bakunin*. Glencoe, Illinois: Free Press, 1953.

Kropotkin, Peter. *Fields, Factories and Workshops*. Various editions; New York: Putnam, 1913.

Kropotkin, Peter. *Mutual Aid as a Factor in Evolution*. Various editions; New York: Knopf, 1917.

Kropotkin, Peter. *Conquest of Bread*. New York: Vanguard, 1926. Other editions.

Stirner, Max (S.T. Byington, translator). *The Ego and His Own*. New York: B.R. Tucker, 1907.

In the United States:

Berkman, Alexander. *The ABC's of Anarchism*. London: Freedom Press, current edition; others.

Goldman, Emma. *Anarchism and Other Essays*. New York: Mother Earth Publishing Assoc., 1917.

Andrews, Stephen Pearl. *The Science of Society* (2 parts). New York: Fowler and Wells, 1851, 2,3,4. Other editions at various times and places, last one known in USA, 1888; only current edition available in India, Bombay: Free Economic Review, Arya Bhavan, Sandhurst road, Bombay 4.

Warren, Josiah. *True Civilization*. Princeton, Mass., 1875. Several other previous editions, above last known in this country, under auspices of E.H. Heywood.

Tucker, Benjamin R. *Instead of a Book, by a Man Too Busy to Write One*. New York: B.R. Tucker, 1893.

Walker, James L. *The Philosophy of Egoism.* Denver: Katharine L. Walker, 1905. (The USA Stirner.)

While on the subject of political Marxism, if you liked the Crossman edition *The God That Failed* you could try Talmadge. If you still have illusions about the Worker's Fatherland try Gordon and Berneri. A wonderful example of how an American came to embrace Stalinism is Freeman; a superlative one on how an American got disenchanted, in a period when it was not "smart" to be an "ex-Red," is Fred Beal. Some good criticism in Parkes.

Talmadge, Irving (ed.). *Whose Revolution?* New York: Howell, Soskin, 1941.

Gordon, Manya. *Workers Before and After Lenin.* New York: Dutton, 1941.

Berneri, Marie Louise. *Workers in Stalin's Russia.* London: Freedom Press, several printings.

Freeman, Joseph. *An American Testament.* New York: Farrar, 1936.

Beal, Fred. *Proletarian Journey.* New York: Hillman, Curl, 1937.

Parkes, Henry Bamford. *Marxism: An Autopsy.* Boston: Houghton, Mifflin, 1939.

Two books on the scene of world-wide scale for the past 25 years. Tough and most readable. Folks with the "objective"-type prejudices and biases have been fervently denouncing these two authors and their books for a decade or more; try reading them instead of joining the howling pack for a change.

Burnham, James. *The Managerial Revolution.* New York: John Day, 1941.

Dennis, Lawrence. *The Dynamics of War and Revolution.* New York: Weekly Foreign Letter, 1940. (Note: Dennis' earlier books, *Is Capitalism Doomed?* [1932] and *The Coming American Fascism* [1936] still have plenty of material which is most pertinent in examining current world trends; all of his books were greeted with rave reviews, but his fair-minded "objective" enemies long ago smeared him as a "lunatic" and "crackpot.")

This one started Senator McCarthy on his way to the political shooting gallery; attacking political generals has always been risky business. How this got published will probably forever mystify General Marshall's adoring circle. A real burnable item for the future.

McCarthy, Joseph R. (Senator). *America's Retreat from Victory : The Story of George Catlett Marshall*. New York: Devin-Adair, 1952.

A great pamphleteer and controversialist, with a writing style few can approach for lucidity. A file of his famous broadsheet *Analysis* (1944-1951) will one day be the object of wide search. Everything he has written deserves incineration.

Chodorov, Frank. *The Myth of the Post Office*. Chicago: Henry Regnery, 1948. *One Is A Crowd: Reflections of An Individualist*. New York: Devin-Adair, 1952. *The Income Tax, Root of All Evil*. New York: Devin-Adair, 1953.

For those accustomed to reading canonical accounts of their favorite politicians, the following are recommended as a sample change of diet, calculated to bring grimaces depending upon whose idol is subject to the probe; there are plenty more like these. But I doubt if they will budge the Carlyle tradition of worship of Great Men very much. (As an afterthought, you could also try W.G. Clugston, *Rascals in Democracy*. (New York: R.R. Smith, 1940.)

Seldes, George. *Sawdust Caesar* (Mussolini). New York: Harper, 1935.

Heiden, Konrad. *Der Fuehrer* (Hitler). New York: Knopf, 1936.

Souvarine, Boris. *Stalin*. New York: Alliance, 1939.

Flynn, John T. *The Roosevelt Myth*. New York: Devin-Adair, 1948.

MacDonald, Dwight. *Henry Wallace*. New York: Vanguard, 1948.

Hughes, Emrys. *Winston Churchill in War and Peace*. Glasgow, Scotland: Unity Pub. Co., 1950. USA revised edition coming; New York: Exposition Press, 1955.

Neilson, Francis. *The Churchill Legend*. Appleton, Wis.: C.C. Nelson Pub. Co., 1954.

A brief selection of disturbing literature for militarists, lovers of war and uncritical exponents of the virtuousness of violence; Owen and Trumbo are included specially for those who thought Erich Maria Remarque's *All Quiet on the Western Front* was depressing.

Olday, John. *The March to Death*. London: Freedom Press, 1943.

Hamlin, C.H. *The War Myth in the United States*. New York: Vanguard, 1927.

Butler, Smedley D. *War is a Racket*. New York: Round Table Press, 1935.

Sherwood, Robert. *Idiot's Delight*. New York: Scribners, 1937.

Trumbo, Dalton. *Johnny Got His Gun*. Philadelphia: Lippincott, 1939.

Owen, Walter. *The Cross of Carl: An Allegory*. Boston: Little, Brown, 1931.

Seldes, George. *Iron, Blood and Profits*. New York: Harper, 1934.

Engelbrecht, H.C., and Hanighen, Frank. *Merchants of Death*. New York: Dodd, 1934.

Huie, William Bradford. *The Execution of Private Slovik*. New York: Signet Pocket Books, 1954.

Hasek, Jaroslav. *The Good Soldier Schweik*. Several editions.

Hirschfeld, Magnus. *The Sexual History of the World War*. New York: Cadillac Publishing Co., 1941.

A symposium of literature dealing with the origins of the two world wars and their consequences. This is the most important issue in the world today, and completely blots out the domestic problem and quarrels of our day as far as urgency is concerned. There is a prodigious official apologia already established which controls the source of most attitudes the great majority hold right now. The books listed below are offered as counterweights to the official "line" on these matters. Reading them may "unbalance" you and make you "prejudiced" and "biased."

1. For the propaganda of the first war, and the part played by diplomats, historians, clergymen, businessmen (see titles 7 and 8, above) and others in "selling" us on the whole affair; they may adjust a few of your fixations, especially those dealing with the alleged inno-

cence of the Russo-Franco-Anglo-American Allies, since you are no doubt sure that the side that lost was the haven of the sinners. Try Keynes if you think the peace treaty had nothing to do with the next war.

Neilson, Francis. *How Diplomats Make War.* New York: Viking, 1916.

Barnes, Harry Elmer. *In Quest of Truth and Justice.* Chicago: Nat. Hist. Society, 1929.

Barnes, Harry Elmer. *The Genesis of the World War.* third edition. New York: Knopf, 1929.

Grattan, C. Hartley. "The Historians Cut Loose," *American Mercury,* August, 1927; also in above.

Peterson, H.C. *Propaganda for War.* Norman, Okla.: Univ. of Oklahoma Press, 1939.

Viereck, George Sylvester. *Spreading Germs of Hate.* New York: Liveright, 1930.

Ponsonby, Arthur. *Falsehood in Wartime.* New York: Dutton, 1929.

Abrams, Ray Hamilton. *Preachers Present Arms.* New York: Round Table Press, 1933.

Keynes, John Maynard. *The Economic Consequences of the Peace.* New York: Harcourt, 1920.

A wonderful antidote for those who have become mesmerized by modern pin-up diplomats and the conduct of international policy with brass band and loud speaker accompaniment:

Huddleston, Sisley. *Popular Diplomacy and War.* West Rindge, N.H.: Richard R. Smith Publisher, Inc., 1954.

Of course, the "objective" histories of what happened during the Russian and Spanish revolutions are in, but the following constitute part of the case of the non-Communist but libertarian left factions, which are usually carefully steered past, due to the embarrassing questions they pose.

Richards, Vernon. *Lessons of the Spanish Revolution.* London: Freedom Press, 1953.

Voline, V.M. Eichenbaum. *Nineteen Seventeen: The Russian Revolution Betrayed.* New York: Libertarian Book Club, 1954.

2. On the world events of 1933-47 your opinions were probably frozen into their current shape by the accounts of the virgin purity of the intentions and actions of the winners and the necessity and wisdom of everything done by them. Here are a few burnable items for the dissenting side. Hitler and Mussolini and the Japs did it all, and the allies were blameless once more? Stalin, the FDR administration and Churchill's lads were innocent of other intents than sponsoring the cause of world virtue? Give the following a serious consideration; they can't *all* be brushed off.

Neilson, Francis. *The Makers of War.* Appleton, Wisc.: C.C. Nelson Pub. Co., 1950.

Sargent, Porter. *Getting US Into War.* Boston: Porter Sargent, 1941.

Barnes, Harry Elmer. *The Struggle Against the Historical Blackout.* Ninth edition, n.p., 1951.

Morgenstern, George. *Pearl Harbor: The Story of the Secret War.* New York: Devin-Adair, 1947.

Theobald, Adm. Robert A. *The Final Secret of Pearl Harbor.* New York: Devin-Adair, 1954.

Current, Richard N. *Secretary Stimson: A Study in Statecraft.* New Brunswick, N.J.: Rutgers Univ. Press, 1954.

Sanborn, Frederic R. *Design for War.* New York: Devin-Adair, 1951.

Chamberlin, William H. *America's Second Crusade.* Chicago: Regnery, 1950.

Tansill, Charles C. *Back Door to War.* Chicago: Regnery, 1952.

Bonus if you can find it. this item below was banned in this country: a blueprint for what later was done:

Rogerson, Sidney. *Propaganda For the Next War.* London: Geoffrey Bles, 1938. (Note: Charles A. Beard's *President Roosevelt and the Coming of the War, 1941* is an obvious candidate for the burning bin in this department; the original attention it received inclined me to omit it from this less well-known group.)

3. Some footnotes on the domestic scene during the war; the Pacific Coast Japanese got a fair shake? The administration's sedition trial was smart? We had no victims of political persecution and developed

no totalitarian trends ourselves? Check these:

Renne, Louis Obed. *Our Day of Empire*. Glasgow, Scotland: The Strickland Press, 1954.

Grodzins, Morton. *Americans Betrayed*. Chicago: Univ. of Chicago Press, 1949.

Dennis, Lawrence, and St. George, Maximilian. *A Trial on Trial*. New York: National Civil Rights Committee, 1945.

Viereck, George Sylvester. *Men Into Beasts*. New York: Gold Medal Pocket Books, 1952.

Flynn, John T. *As We Go Marching*. New York: Doubleday, 1944.

4. The conduct of the war and the postwar settlement are monoliths of rectitude? The German and Japanese war criminals (i.e., the losers) were dealt with fairly and the winners were not guilty of doing exactly the same? Go over the following carefully:

Reel, A. Frank. *The Case of General Yamashita*. Chicago: University of Chicago Press, 1949.

Belgion, Montgomery. *Victor's Justice*. Chicago: Regnery, 1948.

Veale, F.J.P. *Advance to Barbarism*. London: Thompson & Smith, 1948; enlarged ed., Appleton, Wis.: C.C. Nelson, 1953.

Gollancz, Victor. *In Darkest Germany*. Chicago: Regnery, 1946.

Gollancz, Victor. *Our Threatened Values*. Chicago: Regnery, 1948.

Utley, Freda. *The High Cost of Vengeance*. Chicago: Regnery, 1949.

Hankey, Lord. *Politics, Trials and Errors*. Chicago: Regnery, 1950.

Grenfell, Russell. *Unconditional Hatred*. New York: Devin-Adair, 1953.

Wormser, Rene. *The Myth of the Good and Bad Nations*. Chicago: Henry Regnery, 1954.

5. A couple of pointed productions sure to induce a few cases of apoplexy:

Barnes, Harry Elmer. *The Chickens of the Interventionist Liberals Have Come Home to Roost: The Bitter Fruits of Globaloney*. Chicago: Renaissance Book Club, 1953.

Barnes, Harry Elmer (editor). *Perpetual War for Perpetual Peace*.

Caldwell, Idaho: Caxton, 1953.

Who started the fighting in Korea, anyway? If you don't like "revisionism" when applied to the World Wars due to ideological fixations, maybe you would like this variety; this is the North Korean-Chinese-Russian case:

Stone, I.F. *The Hidden History of the Korean War.* New York: Monthly Review Press, 1952.

Marzani, Carl. *We Can Be Friends: Origins of the Cold War.* New York: Topical Book Pub., 1952.

As a semantic aid in understanding the many ways the words you have been reading can be twisted, we can wind up our Manual with a fitting "nightcap":

Bierce, Ambrose. *The Devil's Dictionary.* Several editions; perhaps you could try New York: World Books, 1948.

Nomad, Max. *The Skeptic's Political Dictionary.* New York: American Book Co., 1953.

Index
OF NAMES & AUTHORS